HAMLET

William Shakespeare

TECHNICAL DIRECTOR Maxwell Krohn
EDITORIAL DIRECTOR Justin Kestler
MANAGING EDITOR Ben Florman

SERIES EDITORS Boomie Aglietti, Justin Kestler
PRODUCTION Christian Lorentzen

WRITER Brian Phillips
EDITORS Wendy Cheng, John Crowther

This edition published by Spark Publishing

Spark Publishing
A Division of SparkNotes LLC
120 Fifth Avenue, 8th Floor
New York, NY 10011

02 03 04 05 SN 9 8 7 6 5 4 3 2

Please send all comments and questions or report errors to
feedback@sparknotes.com.

Library of Congress information available upon request

Printed and bound in the United States

RRD-C

ISBN 1-58663-351-1

INTRODUCTION:
A PROLOGUE
FROM THE
BARD

Brave scholars, blessed with time and energy,
    At school, fair Harvard, set about to glean,
From dusty tomes and modern poetry,
    All truths and knowledge formerly unseen.
From forth the hungry minds of these good folk
    Study guides, star-floss'd, soon came to life;
Whose deep and deft analysis awoke
    The latent "A"s of those in lit'rary strife.
Aim far past passing—insight from our trove
    Will free your comprehension from its cage.
Our SparkNotes' worth, online we also prove;
    Behold this book! Same brains, but paper page.
If patient or "whatever," please attend,
    What you have missed, our toil shall strive to mend.

Contents

NOTE: This SparkNote refers to the text of *Hamlet* given in *The Norton Shakespeare*, edited by Stephen Greenblatt. Other editions of the play may differ in line numbering, spelling, punctuation, and diction.

CONTEXT

THE MOST INFLUENTIAL WRITER in all of English literature, William Shakespeare was born in 1564 to a suc-
cessful middle-class glove-maker in Stratford-upon-
Avon, England. Shakespeare attended grammar
school, but his formal education proceeded no further.
In 1582 he married an older woman, Anne Hathaway, and had
three children with her. Around 1590 he left his family behind and
traveled to London to work as an actor and playwright. Public and
critical success quickly followed, and Shakespeare eventually
became the most popular playwright in England and part-owner of
the Globe Theater. His career bridged the reigns of Elizabeth I (ruled
1558–1603) and James I (ruled 1603–1625), and he was a favorite
of both monarchs. Indeed, James granted Shakespeare's company
the greatest possible compliment by bestowing upon its members
the title of King's Men. Wealthy and renowned, Shakespeare retired
to Stratford and died in 1616 at the age of fifty-two. At the time of
Shakespeare's death, literary luminaries such as Ben Jonson hailed
his works as timeless.

Shakespeare's works were collected and printed in various editions in the century following his death, and by the early eighteenth
century his reputation as the greatest poet ever to write in English
was well established. The unprecedented admiration garnered by
his works led to a fierce curiosity about Shakespeare's life, but the
dearth of biographical information has left many details of Shakespeare's personal history shrouded in mystery. Some people have
concluded from this fact that Shakespeare's plays were really written by someone else—Francis Bacon and the Earl of Oxford are the
two most popular candidates—but the support for this claim is
overwhelmingly circumstantial, and the theory is not taken seri-
ously by many scholars.

In the absence of credible evidence to the contrary, Shakespeare
must be viewed as the author of the thirty-seven plays and 154 son-
nets that bear his name. The legacy of this body of work is immense.
A number of Shakespeare's plays seem to have transcended even the
category of brilliance, becoming so influential as to profoundly
affect the course of Western literature and culture ever after.

Written during the first part of the seventeenth century (probably in 1600 or 1601), *Hamlet* was probably first performed in July 1602. It was first published in printed form in 1603 and appeared in an enlarged edition in 1604. As was common practice during the sixteenth and seventeenth centuries, Shakespeare borrowed for his plays ideas and stories from earlier literary works. He could have taken the story of Hamlet from several possible sources, including a twelfth-century Latin history of Denmark compiled by Saxo Grammaticus and a prose work by the French writer François de Belleforest, entitled *Histoires Tragiques*.

The raw material that Shakespeare appropriated in writing Hamlet is the story of a Danish prince whose uncle murders the prince's father, marries his mother, and claims the throne. The prince pretends to be feeble-minded to throw his uncle off guard, then manages to kill his uncle in revenge. Shakespeare changed the emphasis of this story entirely, making his Hamlet a philosophically-minded prince who delays taking action because his knowledge of his uncle's crime is so uncertain. Shakespeare went far beyond making uncertainty a personal quirk of Hamlet's, introducing a number of important ambiguities into the play that even the audience cannot resolve with certainty. For instance, whether Hamlet's mother, Gertrude, shares in Claudius's guilt; whether Hamlet continues to love Ophelia even as he spurns her, in Act III; whether Ophelia's death is suicide or accident; whether the ghost offers reliable knowledge, or seeks to deceive and tempt Hamlet; and, perhaps most importantly, whether Hamlet would be morally justified in taking revenge on his uncle. Shakespeare makes it clear that the stakes riding on some of these questions are enormous—the actions of these characters bring disaster upon an entire kingdom. At the play's end it is not even clear whether justice has been achieved.

By modifying his source materials in this way, Shakespeare was able to take an unremarkable revenge story and make it resonate with the most fundamental themes and problems of the Renaissance. The Renaissance is a vast cultural phenomenon that began in fifteenth-century Italy with the recovery of classical Greek and Latin texts that had been lost to the Middle Ages. The scholars who enthusiastically rediscovered these classical texts were motivated by an educational and political ideal called (in Latin) humanitas—the idea that all of the capabilities and virtues peculiar to human beings should be studied and developed to their furthest extent. Renaissance humanism, as this movement is now called, generated a new interest in human experience, and also an enormous optimism about the potential scope of human understanding. Hamlet's famous speech in Act II, "What a piece of work is a man! How noble in reason, how infinite in faculty, in form and moving how express and admirable, in action how like an angel, in apprehension how like a god—the beauty of the world, the paragon of animals!" (II.ii.293–297) is directly based upon one of the major texts of the Italian humanists, Pico della Mirandola's *Oration on the Dignity of Man*. For the humanists, the purpose of cultivating reason was to lead to a better understanding of how to act, and their fondest hope was that the coordination of action and understanding would lead to great benefits for society as a whole.

As the Renaissance spread to other countries in the sixteenth and seventeenth centuries, however, a more skeptical strain of humanism developed, stressing the limitations of human understanding. For example, the sixteenth-century French humanist, Michel de Montaigne, was no less interested in studying human experiences than the earlier humanists were, but he maintained that the world of experience was a world of appearances, and that human beings could never hope to see past those appearances into the "realities" that lie behind them. This is the world in which Shakespeare places his characters. Hamlet is faced with the difficult task of correcting an injustice that he can never have sufficient knowledge of—a dilemma that is by no means unique, or even uncommon. And while Hamlet is fond of pointing out questions that cannot be answered because they concern supernatural and metaphysical matters, the play as a whole chiefly demonstrates the difficulty of knowing the truth about other people—their guilt or innocence, their motivations, their feelings, their relative states of sanity or insanity. The world of other people is a world of appearances, and *Hamlet* is, fundamentally, a play about the difficulty of living in that world.

PLOT OVERVIEW

O N A DARK WINTER NIGHT, a ghost walks the ramparts of Elsinore Castle in Denmark. Discovered first by a pair of watchmen, then by the scholar Horatio, the ghost resembles the recently deceased King Hamlet, whose brother Claudius has inherited the throne and married the king's widow, Queen Gertrude. When Horatio and the watchmen bring Prince Hamlet, the son of Gertrude and the dead king, to see the ghost, it speaks to him, declaring ominously that it is indeed his father's spirit, and that he was murdered by none other than Claudius. Ordering Hamlet to seek revenge on the man who usurped his throne and married his wife, the ghost disappears with the dawn.

Prince Hamlet devotes himself to avenging his father's death, but, because he is contemplative and thoughtful by nature, he delays, entering into a deep melancholy and even apparent madness. Claudius and Gertrude worry about the prince's erratic behavior and attempt to discover its cause. They employ a pair of Hamlet's friends, Rosencrantz and Guildenstern, to watch him. When Polonius, the pompous Lord Chamberlain, suggests that Hamlet may be mad with love for his daughter, Ophelia, Claudius agrees to spy on Hamlet in conversation with the girl. But though Hamlet certainly seems mad, he does not seem to love Ophelia; he orders her to enter a nunnery and declares that he wishes to ban marriages.

A group of traveling actors comes to Elsinore, and Hamlet seizes upon an idea to test his uncle's guilt. He will have the players perform a scene closely resembling the sequence by which Hamlet imagines his uncle to have murdered his father, so that if Claudius is guilty, he will surely react. When the moment of the murder arrives in the theater, Claudius leaps up and leaves the room. Hamlet and Horatio agree that this proves his guilt. Hamlet goes to kill Claudius but finds him praying. Since he believes that killing Claudius while in prayer would send Claudius's soul to heaven, Hamlet considers that it would be an inadequate revenge and decides to wait. Claudius, now frightened of Hamlet's madness and fearing for his own safety, orders that Hamlet be sent to England at once.

Hamlet goes to confront his mother, in whose bedchamber Polonius has hidden behind a tapestry. Hearing a noise from behind the tapestry, Hamlet believes the king is hiding there. He draws his sword and stabs through the fabric, killing Polonius. For this crime, he is immediately dispatched to England with Rosencrantz and Guildenstern. However, Claudius's plan for Hamlet includes more than banishment, as he has given Rosencrantz and Guildenstern sealed orders for the King of England demanding that Hamlet be put to death.

In the aftermath of her father's death, Ophelia goes mad with grief and drowns in the river. Polonius's son, Laertes, who has been staying in France, returns to Denmark in a rage. Claudius convinces him that Hamlet is to blame for his father's and sister's deaths. When Horatio and the king receive letters from Hamlet indicating that the prince has returned to Denmark after pirates attacked his ship en route to England, Claudius concocts a plan to use Laertes' desire for revenge to secure Hamlet's death. Laertes will fence with Hamlet in innocent sport, but Claudius will poison Laertes' blade so that if he draws blood, Hamlet will die. As a backup plan, the king decides to poison a goblet, which he will give Hamlet to drink should Hamlet score the first or second hits of the match. Hamlet returns to the vicinity of Elsinore just as Ophelia's funeral is taking place. Stricken with grief, he attacks Laertes and declares that he had in fact always loved Ophelia. Back at the castle, he tells Horatio that he believes one must be prepared to die, since death can come at any moment. A foolish courtier named Osric arrives on Claudius's orders to arrange the fencing match between Hamlet and Laertes.

The sword-fighting begins. Hamlet scores the first hit, but declines to drink from the king's proffered goblet. Instead, Gertrude takes a drink from it and is swiftly killed by the poison. Laertes succeeds in wounding Hamlet, though Hamlet does not die of the poison immediately. First, Laertes is cut by his own sword's blade, and, after revealing to Hamlet that Claudius is responsible for the queen's death, he dies from the blade's poison. Hamlet then stabs Claudius through with the poisoned sword and forces him to drink down the rest of the poisoned wine. Claudius dies, and Hamlet dies immediately after achieving his revenge.

At this moment, a Norwegian prince named Fortinbras, who has led an army to Denmark and attacked Poland earlier in the play, enters with ambassadors from England, who report that Rosencrantz and Guildenstern are dead. Fortinbras is stunned by the gruesome sight of the entire royal family lying sprawled on the floor dead. He moves to take power of the kingdom. Horatio, fulfilling Hamlet's last request, tells him Hamlet's tragic story. Fortinbras orders that Hamlet be carried away in a manner befitting a fallen soldier.

CHARACTER LIST

Hamlet   The Prince of Denmark, the title character, and the protagonist. About thirty years old at the start of the play, Hamlet is the son of Queen Gertrude and the late King Hamlet, and the nephew of the present king, Claudius. Hamlet is melancholy, bitter, and cynical, full of hatred for his uncle's scheming and disgust for his mother's sexuality. A reflective and thoughtful young man who has studied at the University of Wittenberg, Hamlet is often indecisive and hesitant, but at other times prone to rash and impulsive acts.

Claudius   The King of Denmark, Hamlet's uncle, and the play's antagonist. The villain of the play, Claudius is a calculating, ambitious politician, driven by his sexual appetites and his lust for power, but he occasionally shows signs of guilt and human feeling—his love for Gertrude, for instance, seems sincere.

Gertrude   The Queen of Denmark, Hamlet's mother, recently married to Claudius. Gertrude loves Hamlet deeply, but she is a shallow, weak woman who seeks affection and status more urgently than moral rectitude or truth.

Polonius   The Lord Chamberlain of Claudius's court, a pompous, conniving old man. Polonius is the father of Laertes and Ophelia.

Horatio   Hamlet's close friend, who studied with the prince at the university in Wittenberg. Horatio is loyal and helpful to Hamlet throughout the play. After Hamlet's death, Horatio remains alive to tell Hamlet's story.

Ophelia   Polonius's daughter, a beautiful young woman with whom Hamlet has been in love. Ophelia is a sweet and innocent young girl, who obeys her father and her brother, Laertes. Dependent on men to tell her how to behave, she gives in to Polonius's schemes to spy on Hamlet. Even in her lapse into madness and death, she remains maidenly, singing songs about flowers and finally drowning in the river amid the flower garlands she had gathered.

Laertes   Polonius's son and Ophelia's brother, a young man who spends much of the play in France. Passionate and quick to action, Laertes is clearly a foil for the reflective Hamlet.

Fortinbras The young Prince of Norway, whose father the king (also named Fortinbras) was killed by Hamlet's father (also named Hamlet). Now Fortinbras wishes to attack Denmark to avenge his father's honor, making him another foil for Prince Hamlet.

The Ghost The specter of Hamlet's recently deceased father. The ghost, who claims to have been murdered by Claudius, calls upon Hamlet to avenge him. However, it is not entirely certain whether the ghost is what it appears to be, or whether it is something else. Hamlet speculates that the ghost might be a devil sent to deceive him and tempt him into murder, and the question of what the ghost is or where it comes from is never definitively resolved.

Rosencrantz and Guildenstern Two slightly bumbling courtiers, former friends of Hamlet from Wittenberg, who are summoned by Claudius and Gertrude to discover the cause of Hamlet's strange behavior.

Osric   The foolish courtier who summons Hamlet to his duel with Laertes.

Voltimand and Cornelius Courtiers whom Claudius sends to
Norway to persuade the king to prevent Fortinbras
from attacking.

Marcellus and Bernardo The officers who first see the ghost
walking the ramparts of Elsinore and who summon
Horatio to witness it. Marcellus is present when
Hamlet first encounters the ghost.

Francisco A soldier and guardsman at Elsinore.

Reynaldo Polonius's servant, who is sent to France by Polonius to
check up on and spy on Laertes.

ANALYSIS OF MAJOR CHARACTERS

HAMLET

Hamlet has fascinated audiences and readers for centuries, and the first thing to point out about him is that he is enigmatic. There is always more to him than the other characters in the play can figure out; even the most careful and clever readers come away with the sense that they don't know everything there is to know about this character. Hamlet actually tells other characters that there is more to him than meets the eye—notably, his mother, and Rosencrantz and Guildenstern—but his fascination involves much more than this. When he speaks, he sounds as if there's something important he's not saying, maybe something even he is not aware of. The ability to write soliloquies and dialogues that create this effect is one of Shakespeare's most impressive achievements.

A university student whose studies are interrupted by his father's death, Hamlet is extremely philosophical and contemplative. He is particularly drawn to difficult questions or questions that cannot be answered with any certainty. Faced with evidence that his uncle murdered his father, evidence that any other character in a play would believe, Hamlet becomes obsessed with proving his uncle's guilt before trying to act. The standard of "beyond a reasonable doubt" is simply unacceptable to him. He is equally plagued with questions about the afterlife, about the wisdom of suicide, about what happens to bodies after they die—the list is extensive.

But even though he is thoughtful to the point of obsession, Hamlet also behaves rashly and impulsively. When he does act, it is with surprising swiftness and little or no premeditation, as when he stabs Polonius through a curtain without even checking to see who he is. He seems to step very easily into the role of a madman, behaving erratically and upsetting the other characters with his wild speech and pointed innuendos.

It is also important to note that Hamlet is extremely melancholy and discontented with the state of affairs in Denmark and in his own family—indeed, in the world at large. He is extremely disappointed with his mother for marrying his uncle so quickly, and he repudiates Ophelia, a woman he once claimed to love, in the harshest terms. His words often indicate his disgust with and distrust of women in general. At a number of points in the play, he contemplates his own death and even the option of suicide.

But, despite all of the things with which Hamlet professes dissatisfaction, it is remarkable that the prince and heir apparent of Denmark should think about these problems only in personal and philosophical terms. He spends relatively little time thinking about the threats to Denmark's national security from without or the threats to its stability from within (some of which he helps to create through his own carelessness).

CLAUDIUS

Hamlet's major antagonist is a shrewd, lustful, conniving king who contrasts sharply with the other male characters in the play. Whereas most of the other important men in *Hamlet* are preoccupied with ideas of justice, revenge, and moral balance, Claudius is bent upon maintaining his own power. The old King Hamlet was apparently a stern warrior, but Claudius is a corrupt politician whose main weapon is his ability to manipulate others through his skillful use of language. Claudius's speech is compared to poison being poured in the ear—the method he used to murder Hamlet's father. Claudius's love for Gertrude may be sincere, but it also seems likely that he married her as a strategic move, to help him win the throne away from Hamlet after the death of the king. As the play progresses, Claudius's mounting fear of Hamlet's insanity leads him to ever greater self-preoccupation; when Gertrude tells him that Hamlet has killed Polonius, Claudius does not remark that Gertrude might have been in danger, but only that he would have been in danger had he been in the room. He tells Laertes the same thing as he attempts to soothe the young man's anger after his father's death. Claudius is ultimately too crafty for his own good. In Act V, scene ii, rather than allowing Laertes only two methods of killing Hamlet, the sharpened sword and the poison on the blade, Claudius insists on a third, the poisoned goblet. When Gertrude inadvertently drinks the poison and dies, Hamlet is at last able to bring himself to kill Claudius, and the king is felled by his own cowardly machination.

GERTRUDE

Few Shakespearean characters have caused as much uncertainty as Gertrude, the beautiful Queen of Denmark. The play seems to raise more questions about Gertrude than it answers, including: Was she involved with Claudius before the death of her husband? Did she love her husband? Did she know about Claudius's plan to commit the murder? Did she love Claudius, or did she marry him simply to keep her high station in Denmark? Does she believe Hamlet when he insists that he is not mad, or does she pretend to believe him simply to protect herself? Does she intentionally betray Hamlet to Claudius, or does she believe that she is protecting her son's secret?

These questions can be answered in numerous ways, depending upon one's reading of the play. The Gertrude who does emerge clearly in *Hamlet* is a woman defined by her desire for station and affection, as well as by her tendency to use men to fulfill her instinct for self-preservation—which, of course, makes her extremely dependent upon the men in her life. Hamlet's most famous comment about Gertrude is his furious condemnation of women in general: "Frailty, thy name is woman!" (I.ii.146). This comment is as much indicative of Hamlet's agonized state of mind as of anything else, but to a great extent Gertrude does seem morally frail. She never exhibits the ability to think critically about her situation, but seems merely to move instinctively toward seemingly safe choices, as when she immediately runs to Claudius after her confrontation with Hamlet. She is at her best in social situations (I.ii and V.ii), when her natural grace and charm seem to indicate a rich, rounded personality. At times it seems that her grace and charm are her *only* characteristics, and her reliance on men appears to be her sole way of capitalizing on her abilities.

THEMES, MOTIFS & SYMBOLS

THEMES

Themes are the fundamental and often universal ideas explored in a literary work.

THE IMPOSSIBILITY OF CERTAINTY

What separates *Hamlet* from other revenge plays (and maybe from every play written before it) is that the action we expect to see, particularly from Hamlet himself, is continually postponed while Hamlet tries to obtain more certain knowledge about what he is doing. This play poses many questions that other plays would simply take for granted. Can we have certain knowledge about ghosts? Is the ghost what it appears to be, or is it really a misleading fiend? Does the ghost have reliable knowledge about its own death, or is the ghost itself deluded? Moving to more earthly matters: How can we know for certain the facts about a crime that has no witnesses? Can Hamlet know the state of Claudius's soul by watching his behavior? If so, can he know the facts of what Claudius did by observing the state of his soul? Can Claudius (or the audience) know the state of Hamlet's mind by observing his behavior and listening to his speech? Can we know whether our actions will have the consequences we want them to have? Can we know anything about the afterlife?

Many people have seen *Hamlet* as a play about indecisiveness, and thus about Hamlet's failure to act appropriately. It might be more interesting to consider that the play shows us how many uncertainties our lives are built upon, how many unknown quantities are taken for granted when people act or when they evaluate one another's actions.

THE COMPLEXITY OF ACTION

Directly related to the theme of certainty is the theme of action. How is it possible to take reasonable, effective, purposeful action? In *Hamlet*, the question of how to act is affected not only by rational considerations, such as the need for certainty, but also by emo-

15

tional, ethical, and psychological factors. Hamlet himself appears to distrust the idea that it's even possible to act in a controlled, purposeful way. When he does act, he prefers to do it blindly, recklessly, and violently. The other characters obviously think much less about "action" in the abstract than Hamlet does, and are therefore less troubled about the possibility of acting effectively. They simply act as they feel is appropriate. But in some sense they prove that Hamlet is right, because all of their actions miscarry. Claudius possesses himself of queen and crown through bold action, but his conscience torments him, and he is beset by threats to his authority (and, of course, he dies). Laertes resolves that nothing will distract him from acting out his revenge, but he is easily influenced and manipulated into serving Claudius's ends, and his poisoned rapier is turned back upon himself.

THE MYSTERY OF DEATH

In the aftermath of his father's murder, Hamlet is obsessed with the idea of death, and over the course of the play he considers death from a great many perspectives. He ponders both the spiritual aftermath of death, embodied in the ghost, and the physical remainders of the dead, such as by Yorick's skull and the decaying corpses in the cemetery. Throughout, the idea of death is closely tied to the themes of spirituality, truth, and uncertainty in that death may bring the answers to Hamlet's deepest questions, ending once and for all the problem of trying to determine truth in an ambiguous world. And, since death is both the cause and the consequence of revenge, it is intimately tied to the theme of revenge and justice—Claudius's murder of King Hamlet initiates Hamlet's quest for revenge, and Claudius's death is the end of that quest.

The question of his own death plagues Hamlet as well, as he repeatedly contemplates whether or not suicide is a morally legitimate action in an unbearably painful world. Hamlet's grief and misery is such that he frequently longs for death to end his suffering, but he fears that if he commits suicide, he will be consigned to eternal suffering in hell because of the Christian religion's prohibition of suicide. In his famous "To be or not to be" soliloquy (III.i), Hamlet philosophically concludes that no one would choose to endure the pain of life if he or she were not afraid of what will come after death, and that it is this fear which causes complex moral considerations to interfere with the capacity for action.

The Nation as a Diseased Body

Everything is connected in *Hamlet,* including the welfare of the royal family and the health of the state as a whole. The play's early scenes explore the sense of anxiety and dread that surrounds the transfer of power from one ruler to the next. Throughout the play, characters draw explicit connections between the moral legitimacy of a ruler and the health of the nation. Denmark is frequently described as a physical body made ill by the moral corruption of Claudius and Gertrude, and many observers interpret the presence of the ghost as a supernatural omen indicating that "[s]omething is rotten in the state of Denmark" (I.iv.67). The dead King Hamlet is portrayed as a strong, forthright ruler under whose guard the state was in good health, while Claudius, a wicked politician, has corrupted and compromised Denmark to satisfy his own appetites. At the end of the play, the rise to power of the upright Fortinbras suggests that Denmark will be strengthened once again.

Motifs

Motifs are recurring structures, contrasts, or literary devices that can help to develop and inform the text's major themes.

Incest and Incestuous Desire

The motif of incest runs throughout the play and is frequently alluded to by Hamlet and the ghost, most obviously in conversations about Gertrude and Claudius, the former brother-in-law and sister-in-law who are now married. A subtle motif of incestuous desire can be found in the relationship of Laertes and Ophelia, as Laertes sometimes speaks to his sister in suggestively sexual terms and, at her funeral, leaps into her grave to hold her in his arms. However, the strongest overtones of incestuous desire arise in the relationship of Hamlet and Gertrude, in Hamlet's fixation on Gertrude's sex life with Claudius and his preoccupation with her in general.

Misogyny

Shattered by his mother's decision to marry Claudius so soon after her husband's death, Hamlet becomes cynical about women in general, showing a particular obsession with what he perceives to be a connection between female sexuality and moral corruption. This motif of misogyny, or hatred of women, occurs sporadically throughout the play, but it is an important inhibiting factor in Hamlet's relationships with Ophelia and Gertrude. He urges Ophelia to go to a nunnery rather than experience the corruptions of sexuality and exclaims of Gertrude, "Frailty, thy name is woman" (I.ii.146).

EARS AND HEARING

One facet of *Hamlet*'s exploration of the difficulty of attaining true knowledge is slipperiness of language. Words are used to communicate ideas, but they can also be used to distort the truth, manipulate other people, and serve as tools in corrupt quests for power. Claudius, the shrewd politician, is the most obvious example of a man who manipulates words to enhance his own power. The sinister uses of words are represented by images of ears and hearing, from Claudius's murder of the king by pouring poison into his ear to Hamlet's claim to Horatio that "I have words to speak in thine ear will make thee dumb" (IV.vi.21). The poison poured in the king's ear by Claudius is used by the ghost to symbolize the corrosive effect of Claudius's dishonesty on the health of Denmark. Declaring that the story that he was killed by a snake is a lie, he says that "the whole ear of Denmark" is "Rankly abused. . . ." (I.v.36–38).

SYMBOLS

> *Symbols are objects, characters, figures, or colors used to represent abstract ideas or concepts.*

YORICK'S SKULL

In *Hamlet,* physical objects are rarely used to represent thematic ideas. One important exception is Yorick's skull, which Hamlet discovers in the graveyard in the first scene of Act V. As Hamlet speaks to the skull and about the skull of the king's former jester, he fixates on death's inevitability and the disintegration of the body. He urges the skull to "get you to my lady's chamber, and tell her, let her paint an inch thick, to this favor she must come"—no one can avoid death (V.i.178–179). He traces the skull's mouth and says, "Here hung those lips that I have kissed I know not how oft," indicating his fascination with the physical consequences of death (V.i.174–175). This latter idea is an important motif throughout the play, as Hamlet frequently makes comments referring to every human body's eventual decay, noting that Polonius will be eaten by worms, that even kings are eaten by worms, and that dust from the decayed body of Alexander the Great might be used to stop a hole in a beer barrel.

SUMMARY & ANALYSIS

ACT I, SCENE I

SUMMARY
On a dark winter night outside Elsinore Castle in Denmark, an officer named Bernardo comes to relieve the watchman Francisco. In the heavy darkness, the men cannot see each other. Bernardo hears a footstep near him and cries, "Who's there?" After both men ensure that the other is also a watchman, they relax. Cold, tired, and apprehensive from his many hours of guarding the castle, Francisco thanks Bernardo and prepares to go home and go to bed.

Shortly thereafter, Bernardo is joined by Marcellus, another watchman, and Horatio, a friend of Prince Hamlet. Bernardo and Marcellus have urged Horatio to stand watch with them, because they believe they have something shocking to show him. In hushed tones, the they discuss the apparition they have seen for the past two nights, and which they now hope to show Horatio: the ghost of the recently deceased King Hamlet, which they claim has appeared before them on the castle ramparts in the late hours of the night.

Horatio is skeptical, but then the ghost suddenly appears before the men and just as suddenly vanishes. Terrified, Horatio acknowledges that the specter does indeed resemble the dead King of Denmark, that it even wears the armor King Hamlet wore when he battled against the armies of Norway, and the same frown he wore when he fought against the Poles. Horatio declares that the ghost must bring warning of impending misfortune for Denmark, perhaps in the form of a military attack. He recounts the story of King Hamlet's conquest of certain lands once belonging to Norway, saying that Fortinbras, the young prince of Norway, now seeks to reconquer those forfeited lands.

The ghost materializes for a second time, and Horatio tries to speak to it. The ghost remains silent, however, and disappears again just as the cock crows at the first hint of dawn. Horatio suggests that they tell Prince Hamlet, the dead king's son, about the apparition. He believes that though the ghost did not speak to him, if it is really the ghost of King Hamlet, it will not refuse to speak to his beloved son.

ANALYSIS

Hamlet was written around the year 1600 in the final years of the reign of Queen Elizabeth I, who had been the monarch of England for more than forty years and was then in her late sixties. The prospect of Elizabeth's death and the question of who would succeed her was a subject of grave anxiety at the time, since Elizabeth had no children, and the only person with a legitimate royal claim, James of Scotland, was the son of Mary, Queen of Scots, and therefore represented a political faction to which Elizabeth was opposed. (When Elizabeth died in 1603, James did inherit the throne, becoming King James I.)

It is no surprise, then, that many of Shakespeare's plays from this period, including *Hamlet*, concern transfers of power from one monarch to the next. These plays focus particularly on the uncertainties, betrayals, and upheavals that accompany such shifts in power, and the general sense of anxiety and fear that surround them. The situation Shakespeare presents at the beginning of *Hamlet* is that a strong and beloved king has died, and the throne has been inherited not by his son, as we might expect, but by his brother. Still grieving the old king, no one knows yet what to expect from the new one, and the guards outside the castle are fearful and suspicious.

The supernatural appearance of the ghost on a chilling, misty night outside Elsinore Castle indicates immediately that something is wrong in Denmark. The ghost serves to enlarge the shadow King Hamlet casts across Denmark, indicating that something about his death has upset the balance of nature. The appearance of the ghost also gives physical form to the fearful anxiety that surrounds the transfer of power after the king's death, seeming to imply that the future of Denmark is a dark and frightening one. Horatio in particular sees the ghost as an ill omen boding violence and turmoil in Denmark's future, comparing it to the supernatural omens that supposedly presaged the assassination of Julius Caesar in ancient Rome (and which Shakespeare had recently represented in *Julius Caesar*). Since Horatio proves to be right, and the appearance of the ghost does presage the later tragedies of the play, the ghost functions as a kind of internal foreshadowing, implying tragedy not only to the audience but to the characters as well.

The scene also introduces the character of Horatio, who, with the exception of the ghost, is the only major character in the scene. Without sacrificing the forward flow of action or breaking the atmosphere of dread, Shakespeare establishes that Horatio is a good-humored man who is also educated, intelligent, and skeptical of supernatural events. Before he sees the ghost, he insists, "Tush, tush, 'twill not appear" (I.i.29). Even after seeing it, he is reluctant to give full credence to stories of magic and mysticism. When Marcellus says that he has heard that the crowing of the cock has the power to dispel evil powers, so that "[n]o fairy takes, nor witch hath power to charm," Horatio replies, "So have I heard, and do in part believe it," emphasizing the "in part" (I.i.144–146).

But Horatio is not a blind rationalist, either, and when he sees the ghost, he does not deny its existence—on the contrary, he is overwhelmed with terror. His ability to accept the truth at once even when his predictions have been proved wrong indicates the fundamental trustworthiness of his character. His reaction to the ghost functions to overcome the audience's sense of disbelief, since for a man as skeptical, intelligent, and trustworthy as Horatio to believe in and fear the ghost is far more impressive and convincing than if its only witnesses had been a pair of superstitious watchmen. In this subtle way, Shakespeare uses Horatio to represent the audience's perspective throughout this scene. By overcoming Horatio's skeptical resistance, the ghost gains the audience's suspension of disbelief as well.

ACT I, SCENE II

SUMMARY

The morning after Horatio and the guardsmen see the ghost, King Claudius gives a speech to his courtiers, explaining his recent marriage to Gertrude, his brother's widow and the mother of Prince Hamlet. Claudius says that he mourns his brother but has chosen to balance Denmark's mourning with the delight of his marriage. He mentions that young Fortinbras has written to him, rashly demanding the surrender of the lands King Hamlet won from Fortinbras's father, and dispatches Cornelius and Voltimand with a message for the King of Norway, Fortinbras's elderly uncle.

His speech concluded, Claudius turns to Laertes, the son of the Lord Chamberlain, Polonius. Laertes expresses his desire to return to France, where he was staying before his return to Denmark for Claudius's coronation. Polonius gives his son permission, and Claudius jovially grants Laertes his consent as well.

Turning to Prince Hamlet, Claudius asks why "the clouds still hang" upon him, as Hamlet is still wearing black mourning clothes (I.ii.66). Gertrude urges him to cast off his "nightly colour," but he replies bitterly that his inner sorrow is so great that his dour appearance is merely a poor mirror of it (I.ii.68). Affecting a tone of fatherly advice, Claudius declares that all fathers die, and all sons must lose their fathers. When a son loses a father, he is duty-bound to mourn, but to mourn for too long is unmanly and inappropriate. Claudius urges Hamlet to think of him as a father, reminding the prince that he stands in line to succeed to the throne upon Claudius's death.

With this in mind, Claudius says that he does not wish for Hamlet to return to school at Wittenberg (where he had been studying before his father's death), as Hamlet has asked to do. Gertrude echoes her husband, professing a desire for Hamlet to remain close to her. Hamlet stiffly agrees to obey her. Claudius claims to be so pleased by Hamlet's decision to stay that he will celebrate with festivities and cannon fire, an old custom called "the king's rouse." Ordering Gertrude to follow him, he escorts her from the room, and the court follows.

Alone, Hamlet exclaims that he wishes he could die, that he could evaporate and cease to exist. He wishes bitterly that God had not made suicide a sin. Anguished, he laments his father's death and his mother's hasty marriage to his uncle. He remembers how deeply in love his parents seemed, and he curses the thought that now, not yet two month after his father's death, his mother has married his father's far inferior brother.

> O God! a beast that wants discourse of reason,
> Would have mourn'd longer,—married with mine uncle,
> My father's brother; but no more like my father
> Than I to Hercules: within a month;
> Ere yet the salt of most unrighteous tears
> Had left the flushing in her galled eyes,
> She married:— O, most wicked speed, to post
> With such dexterity to incestuous sheets!
>
> (I.II.150–157)

(See QUOTATIONS, p. 61)

Hamlet quiets suddenly as Horatio strides into the room, followed by Marcellus and Bernardo. Horatio was a close friend of Hamlet at the university in Wittenberg, and Hamlet, happy to see him, asks why he has left the school to travel to Denmark. Horatio says that he came to see King Hamlet's funeral, to which Hamlet curtly replies that Horatio came to see his mother's wedding. Horatio agrees that the one followed closely on the heels of the other. He then tells Hamlet that he, Marcellus, and Bernardo have seen what appears to be his father's ghost. Stunned, Hamlet agrees to keep watch with them that night, in the hope that he will be able to speak to the apparition.

ANALYSIS

Having established a dark, ghostly atmosphere in the first scene, Shakespeare devotes the second to the seemingly jovial court of the recently crowned King Claudius. If the area outside the castle is murky with the aura of dread and anxiety, the rooms inside the castle are devoted to an energetic attempt to banish that aura, as the king, the queen, and the courtiers desperately pretend that nothing is out of the ordinary. It is difficult to imagine a more convoluted family dynamic or a more out-of-balance political situation, but Claudius nevertheless preaches an ethic of balance to his courtiers, pledging to sustain and combine the sorrow he feels for the king's death and the joy he feels for his wedding in equal parts.

But despite Claudius's efforts, the merriment of the court seems superficial. This is largely due to the fact that the idea of balance Claudius pledges to follow is unnatural. How is it possible to balance sorrow for a brother's death with happiness for having married a dead brother's wife? Claudius's speech is full of contradictory words, ideas, and phrases, beginning with "Though yet of Hamlet our late brother's death / The memory be green," which combines the idea of death and decay with the idea of greenery, growth, and renewal (I.ii.1–2). He also speaks of "[o]ur sometime sister, now our queen," "defeated joy," "an auspicious and a dropping eye," "mirth in funeral," and "dirge in marriage" (I.ii.8–12). These ideas sit uneasily with one another, and Shakespeare uses this speech to give his audience an uncomfortable first impression of Claudius. The negative impression is furthered when Claudius affects a fatherly role toward the bereaved Hamlet, advising him to stop grieving for his dead father and adapt to a new life in Denmark. Hamlet obviously does not want Claudius's advice, and Claudius's motives in giving it are thoroughly suspect, since, after all, Hamlet is the man who would have inherited the throne had Claudius not snatched it from him.

The result of all this blatant dishonesty is that this scene portrays as dire a situation in Denmark as the first scene does. Where the first scene illustrated the fear and supernatural danger lurking in Denmark, the second hints at the corruption and weakness of the king and his court. The scene also furthers the idea that Denmark is somehow unsound as a nation, as Claudius declares that Fortinbras makes his battle plans "[h]olding a weak supposal of our worth, / Or thinking by our late dear brother's death / Our state to be disjoint and out of frame" (I.ii.18–20).

Prince Hamlet, devastated by his father's death and betrayed by his mother's marriage, is introduced as the only character who is unwilling to play along with Claudius's gaudy attempt to mimic a healthy royal court. On the one hand, this may suggest that he is the only honest character in the royal court, the only person of high standing whose sensibilities are offended by what has happened in the aftermath of his father's death. On the other hand, it suggests that he is a malcontent, someone who refuses to go along with the rest of the court for the sake of the greater good of stability. In any case, Hamlet already feels, as Marcellus will say later, that "[s]omething is rotten in the state of Denmark" (I.iv.67). We also see that his mother's hasty remarriage has shattered his opinion of womanhood ("Frailty, thy name is woman," he cries out famously in this scene [I.ii.146]), a motif that will develop through his unraveling romantic relationship with Ophelia and his deteriorating relationship with his mother.

His soliloquy about suicide ("O, that this too too solid flesh would melt, / Thaw and resolve itself into a dew!" [I.ii.129–130]) ushers in what will be a central idea in the play. The world is painful to live in, but, within the Christian framework of the play, if one commits suicide to end that pain, one damns oneself to eternal suffering in hell. The question of the moral validity of suicide in an unbearably painful world will haunt the rest of the play; it reaches the height of its urgency in the most famous line in all of English literature: "To be, or not to be: that is the question" (III.i.58). In this scene Hamlet mainly focuses on the appalling conditions of life, railing against Claudius's court as "an unweeded garden, / That grows to seed; things rank and gross in nature / Possess it merely" (I.ii.135–137). Throughout the play, we watch the gradual crumbling of the beliefs on which Hamlet's worldview has been based. Already, in this first soliloquy, religion has failed him, and his warped family situation can offer him no solace.

ACT I, SCENES III–IV

SUMMARY: ACT I, SCENE III

In Polonius's house, Laertes prepares to leave for France. Bidding his sister, Ophelia, farewell, he cautions her against falling in love with Hamlet, who is, according to Laertes, too far above her by birth to be able to love her honorably. Since Hamlet is responsible not only for his own feelings but for his position in the state, it may be impossible for him to marry her. Ophelia agrees to keep Laertes' advice as a "watchman" close to her heart but urges him not to give her advice that he does not practice himself. Laertes reassures her that he will take care of himself.

Polonius enters to bid his son farewell. He tells Laertes that he must hurry to his ship but then delays him by giving him a great deal of advice about how to behave with integrity and practicality. Polonius admonishes Laertes to keep his thoughts to himself, restrain himself from acting on rash desires, and treat people with familiarity but not with vulgarity. He advises him to hold on to his old friends but be slow to embrace new friends; to be slow to quarrel but to fight boldly if the need arises; to listen more than he talks; to dress richly but not gaudily; to refrain from borrowing or lending money; and, finally, to be true to himself above all things.

Laertes leaves, bidding farewell to Ophelia once more. Alone with his daughter, Polonius asks Ophelia what Laertes told her before he left. Ophelia says that it was "something touching the Lord Hamlet" (I.ii.89). Polonius asks her about her relationship with Hamlet. She tells him that Hamlet claims to love her. Polonius sternly echoes Laertes' advice, and forbids Ophelia to associate with Hamlet anymore. He tells her that Hamlet has deceived her in swearing his love, and that she should see through his false vows and rebuff his affections. Ophelia pledges to obey.

SUMMARY: ACT I, SCENE IV

It is now night. Hamlet keeps watch outside the castle with Horatio and Marcellus, waiting in the cold for the ghost to appear. Shortly after midnight, trumpets and gunfire sound from the castle, and Hamlet explains that the new king is spending the night carousing, as is the Danish custom. Disgusted, Hamlet declares that this sort of custom is better broken than kept, saying that the king's revelry makes Denmark a laughingstock among other nations and lessens the Danes' otherwise impressive achievements. Then the ghost appears, and Hamlet calls out to it. The ghost beckons Hamlet to follow it out into the night. His companions urge him not to follow, begging him to consider that the ghost might lead him toward harm.

Hamlet himself is unsure whether his father's apparition is truly the king's spirit or an evil demon, but he declares that he cares nothing for his life and that, if his soul is immortal, the ghost can do nothing to harm his soul. He follows after the apparition and disappears into the darkness. Horatio and Marcellus, stunned, declare that the event bodes ill for the nation. Horatio proclaims that heaven will oversee the outcome of Hamlet's encounter with the ghost, but Marcellus says that they should follow and try to protect him themselves. After a moment, Horatio and Marcellus follow after Hamlet and the ghost.

ANALYSIS: ACT I, SCENES III–IV

> *Neither a borrower nor a lender be:*
> *For loan oft loses both itself and friend;*
> *And borrowing dulls the edge of husbandry.*
>
> (I.III.75–77)
>
> (See QUOTATIONS, p. 63)

The active, headstrong, and affectionate Laertes contrasts powerfully with the contemplative Hamlet, becoming one of Hamlet's most important foils in the play. (A foil is a character who by contrast emphasizes the distinct characteristics of another character.) As the plot progresses, Hamlet's hesitancy to undertake his father's revenge will markedly contrast with Laertes' furious willingness to avenge his father's death (III.iv). Act I, scene iii serves to introduce this contrast. Since the last scene portrayed the bitterly fractured state of Hamlet's family, by comparison, the bustling normalcy of Polonius's household appears all the more striking. Polonius's long speech advising Laertes on how to behave in France is self-consciously paternal, almost excessively so, as if to hammer home the contrast between the fatherly love Laertes enjoys and Hamlet's state of loss and estrangement. Hamlet's conversation with the ghost of his father in Act I, scene v will be a grotesque recapitulation of the father-to-son speech, with vastly darker content.

As in the previous scene, when Claudius and Gertrude advised Hamlet to stay in Denmark and cast off his mourning, the third scene develops through a motif of family members giving one another advice, or orders masked as advice. While Polonius and Laertes seem to have a relatively normal father-son relationship, their relationships with Ophelia seem somewhat troubling. They each assume a position of unquestioned authority over her, Polonius treating his daughter as though her feelings are irrelevant ("Affection! pooh! you speak like a green girl") and Laertes treating her as though her judgment is suspect (I.iii.101). Further, Laertes' speech to Ophelia is laced with forceful sexual imagery, referring to her "chaste treasure open" to Hamlet's "unmaster'd importunity" (I.iii.31–32). Combined with the extremely affectionate interplay between the brother and sister, this sexual imagery creates an incestuous undertone, echoing the incest of Claudius's marriage to his brother's wife and Hamlet's passionate, conflicting feelings for his mother.

The short transitional scene that follows serves a number of important purposes, as Shakespeare begins to construct a unified world out of the various environments of the play. Whereas the play up to this point has been divided into a number of separate settings, this scene begins to blend together elements of different settings. Hamlet, for instance, has been associated with the world inside Elsinore, but he now makes his appearance in the darkness outside it. Likewise, the terror outside the castle so far has been quite separate from the revelry inside, but now the sound of Claudius's carousing leaks through the walls and reaches Hamlet and his companions in the night.

Act I, scene iv also continues the development of the motif of the ill health of Denmark. Hamlet views the king's carousing as a further sign of the state's corruption, commenting that alcohol makes the bad aspects of a person's character overwhelm all of his or her good qualities. And the appearance of the ghost is again seen as a sign of Denmark's decay, this time by Marcellus, who famously declares, "Something is rotten in the state of Denmark" (I.iv.67).

Finally, the reappearance of the still-silent ghost brings with it a return of the theme of spirituality, truth, and uncertainty, or, more specifically, the uncertainty of truth in a world of spiritual ambiguity. Since Hamlet does not know what lies beyond death, he cannot tell whether the ghost is truly his father's spirit or whether it is an evil demon come from hell to tempt him toward destruction. This uncertainty about the spiritual world will lead Hamlet to wrenching considerations of moral truth. These considerations have already been raised by Hamlet's desire to kill himself in Act I, scene ii and will be explored more directly in the scenes to come.

ACT I, SCENE V–ACT II, SCENE I

SUMMARY: ACT I, SCENE V

In the darkness, the ghost speaks to Hamlet, claiming to be his father's spirit, come to rouse Hamlet to revenge his death, a "foul and most unnatural murder" (I.v.25). Hamlet is appalled at the revelation that his father has been murdered, and the ghost tells him that as he slept in his garden, a villain poured poison into his ear—the very villain who now wears his crown, Claudius. Hamlet's worst fears about his uncle are confirmed. "O my prophetic soul!" he cries (I.v.40). The ghost exhorts Hamlet to seek revenge, telling him that Claudius has corrupted Denmark and corrupted Gertrude, having taken her from the pure love of her first marriage and seduced her in the foul lust of their incestuous union. But the ghost urges Hamlet not to act against his mother in any way, telling him to "leave her to heaven" and to the pangs of her own conscience (I.v.86).

As dawn breaks, the ghost disappears. Intensely moved, Hamlet swears to remember and obey the ghost. Horatio and Marcellus arrive upon the scene and frantically ask Hamlet what has happened. Shaken and extremely agitated, he refuses to tell them, and insists that they swear upon his sword not to reveal what they have seen. He tells them further that he may pretend to be a madman, and he makes them swear not to give the slightest hint that they know anything about his motives. Three times the ghost's voice echoes from beneath the ground, proclaiming, "Swear." Horatio and Marcellus take the oath upon Hamlet's sword, and the three men exit toward the castle. As they leave, Hamlet bemoans the responsibility he now carries: "The time is out of joint: O cursed spite / That ever I was born to set it right!" (I.v.189–190).

SUMMARY: ACT II, SCENE I

Polonius dispatches his servant Reynaldo to France with money and written notes for Laertes, also ordering him to inquire about and spy on Laertes' personal life. He gives him explicit directions as to how to pursue his investigations, then sends him on his way. As Reynaldo leaves, Ophelia enters, visibly upset. She tells Polonius that Hamlet, unkempt and wild-eyed, has accosted her. Hamlet grabbed her, held her, and sighed heavily, but did not speak to her. Polonius says that Hamlet must be mad with his love for Ophelia, for she has distanced herself from him ever since Polonius ordered her to do so. Polonius speculates that this lovesickness might be the cause of Hamlet's moodiness, and he hurries out to tell Claudius of his idea.

ANALYSIS: ACT I, SCENE V–ACT II, SCENE I

The ghost's demand for Hamlet to seek revenge upon Claudius is the pivotal event of Act I. It sets the main plot of the play into motion and leads Hamlet to the idea of feigning madness, which becomes his primary mode of interacting with other people for most of the next three acts, as well as a major device Shakespeare uses to develop his character. Most important, it introduces the idea of retributive justice, the notion that sin must be returned with punishment. Claudius has committed a sin, and now, to restore balance to the kingdom, the sin must be punished. The idea of retribution haunts and goads characters throughout the play, functioning as an important motivation for action, spurring Claudius to guilt, Hamlet to the avoidance of suicide, and Laertes to murderous rage after the deaths of Ophelia and Polonius.

While *Hamlet* fits a genre called revenge tragedy, loosely following the form popularized by Thomas Kyd's earlier *Spanish Tragedy,* it is unlike any other revenge tragedy in that it is more concerned with thought and moral questioning than with bloody action. One of the central tensions in the play comes from Hamlet's inability to find any certain moral truths as he works his way toward revenge. Even in his first encounter with the ghost, Hamlet questions the appearances of things around him and worries whether he can trust his perceptions, doubting the authenticity of his father's ghost and its tragic claim. Because he is contemplative to the point of obsession, Hamlet's decision to feign madness, ostensibly in order to keep the other characters from guessing the motive for his behavior, will lead him at times perilously close to actual madness. In fact, it is impossible to say for certain whether or not Hamlet actually does go mad, and, if so, when his act becomes reality. We have already seen that Hamlet, though thoughtful by nature, also has an excitable streak, which makes him erratic, nervous, and unpredictable. In Act I, scene v, as the ghost disappears, Hamlet seems to have too much nervous energy to deal competently with the curious Horatio and

Marcellus. He is already unsure of what to believe and what to do, and the tension of his uncertainty comes out in sprawling wordplay that makes him seem already slightly mad, calling the ghost names such as "truepenny" and "old mole" as it rumbles, "Swear," from beneath the ground (I.v.152, I.v.164).

The short scene that begins Act II is divided into two parts, the first of which involves Polonius's conversation with Reynaldo about Laertes and the second of which involves Polonius's conversation with Ophelia about Hamlet. The scene serves to develop the character of Polonius, who is one of the most intriguing figures in *Hamlet*. Polonius can be interpreted as either a doddering fool or as a cunning manipulator, and he has been portrayed onstage as both. In this scene, as he carefully instructs Reynaldo in the art of snooping, he seems more the manipulator than the fool, though his obvious love of hearing his own voice leads him into some comical misphrasings ("And then, sir, does a this — a does — / what was I about to say? By the mass, I was about to say some / thing. Where did I leave?" [II.i.49–51]).

In his advice to Reynaldo, Polonius explicitly develops one of the themes of *Hamlet*, the idea that words can be used to bend and alter the truth. He explains to Reynaldo how to ask leading questions of Laertes' acquaintances and how to phrase questions in a way that will seem inoffensive. As with Claudius, who manipulated the royal court with his speech in Act I, scene ii, words become a tool for influencing the minds of others and controlling their perception of the truth. Remember that Claudius killed King Hamlet by pouring poison into his ear. Shakespeare continually illustrates that words can function as poison in the ear as well. As the ghost says in Act I, scene v, Claudius has poisoned "the whole ear of Denmark" with his words (I.v.36). The running imagery of ears and hearing serves as an important symbol of the power of words to manipulate the truth.

Polonius's conversation with Ophelia is important for several reasons. First, it illustrates how Hamlet has been behaving since his encounter with the ghost: he has made good on his promise to Horatio and is behaving as a madman. Though we learn about it only through her description, his emotional scene with Ophelia may stem in part from his general plan to feign insanity, and in part from real distress at seeing Ophelia, since she has recently spurned him. In addition, his mother's marriage to Claudius seems to have shattered his opinion of women in general. The conversation also informs the audience that she has obeyed her father's orders and broken off her relationship with Hamlet, confirming her docile nature and dependence on her father to tell her how to behave. And finally, the conversation engenders an important moment for the plot of the play: Polonius's sudden idea that Hamlet's melancholy and strange behavior may be due to his lovesickness for Ophelia. Though Polonius's overly simple theory is obviously insufficient to explain Hamlet's behavior, it does lead to several plot developments in the next few scenes, including Hamlet's disastrous confrontation with Ophelia and Gertrude and Claudius's decision to spy on Hamlet.

Act II, scene ii

Summary

Within the castle, Claudius and Gertrude welcome Rosencrantz and Guildenstern, two of Hamlet's friends from Wittenberg. Increasingly concerned about Hamlet's erratic behavior and his apparent inability to recover from his father's death, the king and queen have summoned his friends to Elsinore in the hope that they might be able to cheer Hamlet out of his melancholy, or at least discover the cause of it. Rosencrantz and Guildenstern agree to investigate, and the queen orders attendants to take them to her "too much changed" son (II.ii.36).

Polonius enters, announcing the return of the ambassadors whom Claudius sent to Norway. Voltimand and Cornelius enter and describe what took place with the aged and ailing king of Norway: the king rebuked Fortinbras for attempting to make war on Denmark, and Fortinbras swore he would never again attack the Danes. The Norwegian king, overjoyed, bequeathed upon Fortinbras a large annuity, and urged him to use the army he had assembled to attack the Poles instead of the Danes. He has therefore sent a request back to Claudius that Prince Fortinbras's armies be allowed safe passage through Denmark on their way to attack the Poles. Relieved to have averted a war with Fortinbras's army, Claudius declares that he will see to this business later. Voltimand and Cornelius leave.

Turning to the subject of Hamlet, Polonius declares, after a wordy preamble, that the prince is mad with love for Ophelia. He shows the king and queen letters and love poems Hamlet has given to Ophelia, and proposes a plan to test his theory. Hamlet often walks alone through the lobby of the castle, and, at such a time, they could hide behind an arras (a curtain or wall hanging) while Ophelia confronts Hamlet, allowing them to see for themselves whether Hamlet's madness really emanates from his love for her. The king declares that they will try the plan. Gertrude notices that Hamlet is approaching, reading from a book as he walks, and Polonius says that he will speak to the prince. Gertrude and Claudius exit, leaving Polonius alone with Hamlet.

Polonius attempts to converse with Hamlet, who appears insane; he calls the old man a "fishmonger" and answers his questions irrationally. But many of Hamlet's seemingly lunatic statements hide barbed observations about Polonius's pomposity and his old age. Polonius comments that while Hamlet is clearly mad, his replies are often "pregnant" with meaning (II.ii.206). He hurries away, determined to arrange the meeting between Hamlet and Ophelia.

As Polonius leaves, Rosencrantz and Guildenstern enter, and Hamlet seems pleased to see them. They discuss Hamlet's unhappiness about recent affairs in Denmark. Hamlet asks why they have come. Sheepishly, the two men claim they have come merely to visit Hamlet, but he sternly declares that he knows that the king and queen sent for them. They confess this to be true, and Hamlet says that he knows why: because he has lost all of his joy and descended into a state of melancholy in which everything (and everyone) appears sterile and worthless.

Rosencrantz smiles and says he wonders how Hamlet will receive a theatrical troupe that is currently traveling toward the castle. The trumpets blow, announcing the arrival of the actors (or "players"). Hamlet tells his friends they are welcome to stay at Elsinore, but that his "uncle-father and aunt-mother" are deceived in his madness. He is mad only some of the time and at other times is sane.

Polonius enters to announce the arrival of the players, who follow him into the room. Hamlet welcomes them and entreats one of them to give him a speech about the fall of Troy and the death of the Trojan king and queen, Priam and Hecuba. Impressed with the player's speech, Hamlet orders Polonius to see them escorted to guestrooms. He announces that the next night they will hear "The Murder of Gonzago" performed, with an additional short speech that he will write himself. Hamlet leaves Rosencrantz and Guildenstern and now stands alone in the room.

He immediately begins cursing himself, bitterly commenting that the player who gave the speech was able to summon a depth of feeling and expression for long-dead figures who mean nothing to him, while Hamlet is unable to take action even with his far more powerful motives. He resolves to devise a trap for Claudius, forcing the king to watch a play whose plot closely resembles the murder of Hamlet's father; if the king is guilty, he thinks, he will surely show some visible sign of guilt when he sees his sin reenacted on stage. Then, Hamlet reasons, he will obtain definitive proof of Claudius's guilt. "The play's the thing," he declares, "wherein I'll catch the conscience of the king" (II.ii.581–582).

ANALYSIS

If Hamlet is merely pretending to be mad, as he suggests, he does almost too good a job of it. His portrayal is so convincing that many critics contend that his already fragile sanity shatters at the sight of his dead father's ghost. However, the acute and cutting observations he makes while supposedly mad support the view that he is only pretending. Importantly, he declares, "I am but mad north-north-west: when the wind is southerly I know a hawk from a handsaw" (II.ii.361–362). That is, he is only "mad" at certain calculated times, and the rest of the time he knows what is what. But he is certainly confused and upset, and his confusion translates into an extraordinarily intense state of mind suggestive of madness.

This scene, by far the longest in the play, includes several important revelations and furthers the development of some of the play's main themes. The scene contains four main parts: Polonius's conversation with Claudius and Gertrude, which includes the discussion with the ambassadors; Hamlet's conversation with Polonius, in which we see Hamlet consciously feigning madness for the first time; Hamlet's reunion with Rosencrantz and Guildenstern; and the scene with the players, followed by Hamlet's concluding soliloquy on the theme of action. These separate plot developments take place in the same location and occur in rapid succession, allowing the audience to compare and contrast their thematic elements.

We have already seen the developing contrast between Hamlet and Laertes. The section involving the Norwegian ambassadors develops another important contrast, this time between Hamlet and Fortinbras. Like Hamlet, Fortinbras is the grieving son of a dead king, a prince whose uncle inherited the throne in his place. But where Hamlet has sunk into despair, contemplation, and indecision, Fortinbras has devoted himself to the pursuit of revenge. This contrast will be explored much more thoroughly later in the play. Here, it is important mainly to note that Fortinbras's uncle has forbidden him to attack Denmark but given him permission to ride through Denmark on his way to attack Poland. This at least suggests the possibility that the King of Norway is trying to trick Claudius into allowing a hostile army into his country. It is notable that Claudius appears indifferent to the fact that a powerful enemy will be riding through his country with a large army in tow. Claudius seems much more worried about Hamlet's madness, indicating that where King Hamlet was a powerful warrior who sought to expand Denmark's power abroad, Claudius is a politician who is more concerned about threats from within his state.

The arrival of Rosencrantz and Guildenstern, two of the most enigmatic figures in Hamlet, is another important development. These two characters are manipulated by all of the members of the royal family and seem to exist in a state of fear that they will offend the wrong person or give away the wrong secret at the wrong time. One of the strangest qualities of the two men is their extraordinary similarity. In fact, Shakespeare leaves Rosencrantz and Guildenstern almost entirely undifferentiated from one another. "Thanks, Rosencrantz and gentle Guildenstern," Claudius says, and Gertrude replies, "Thanks, Guildenstern and gentle Rosencrantz," almost as though it does not matter which is which (II.ii.33–34). The two men's questioning of Hamlet is a parody of a Socratic dialogue. They propose possibilities, develop ideas according to rational argument, and find their attempts to understand Hamlet's behavior entirely thwarted by his uncooperative replies.

> What a piece of work is man! How noble in reason!
> how infinite in faculties! in form and moving, how
> express and admirable! in action how like an angel! in
> apprehension, how like a god! the beauty of the
> world! the paragon of animals! And yet, to me, what
> is this quintessence of dust?   (II.ii.293–298)
> (See QUOTATIONS, p. 65)

The other important event in this scene is the arrival of the players. The presence of players and play-acting within the play points to an important theme: that real life is in certain ways like play-acting. Hamlet professes to be amazed by the player king's ability to engage emotionally with the story he is telling even though it is only an imaginative recreation. Hamlet is prevented from responding to his own situation because he doesn't have certain knowledge about it, but the player king, and theater audiences in general, can respond feelingly even to things they know to be untrue. In fact, most of the time people respond to their real-life situations with feelings and actions that are not based on certain knowledge. This is what Hamlet refuses to do. His refusal to act like he knows what he's doing when he really doesn't may be construed as heroic and appropriate, or quixotic and impossible. In either case, Hamlet's plan to trap the king by eliciting an emotional response is highly unsound: Claudius's feelings about a play could never be construed as a reliable index of its truth.

ACT III, SCENE I

SUMMARY

Claudius and Gertrude discuss Hamlet's behavior with Rosencrantz and Guildenstern, who say they have been unable to learn the cause of his melancholy. They tell the king and queen about Hamlet's enthusiasm for the players. Encouraged, Gertrude and Claudius agree that they will see the play that evening. Rosencrantz and Guildenstern leave, and Claudius orders Gertrude to leave as well, saying that he and Polonius intend to spy on Hamlet's confrontation with Ophelia. Gertrude exits, and Polonius directs Ophelia to walk around the lobby. Polonius hears Hamlet coming, and he and the king hide.

Hamlet enters, speaking thoughtfully and agonizingly to himself about the question of whether to commit suicide to end the pain of experience: "To be, or not to be: that is the question" (III.i.58). He says that the miseries of life are such that no one would willingly bear them, except that they are afraid of "something after death" (III.i.80). Because we do not know what to expect in the afterlife, we would rather "bear those ills we have," Hamlet says, "than fly to others that we know not of" (III.i.83–84). In mid-thought, Hamlet sees Ophelia approaching. Having received her orders from Polonius, she tells him that she wishes to return the tokens of love he has given her. Angrily, Hamlet denies having given her anything; he laments the dishonesty of beauty, and claims both to have loved Ophelia once and never to have loved her at all. Bitterly commenting on the wretchedness of humankind, he urges Ophelia to enter a nunnery rather than become a "breeder of sinners" (III.i.122–123). He criticizes women for making men behave like monsters and for contributing to the world's dishonesty by painting their faces to appear more beautiful than they are. Working himself into a rage, Hamlet denounces Ophelia, women, and humankind in general, saying that he wishes to end all marriages. As he storms out, Ophelia mourns the "noble mind" that has now lapsed into apparent madness (III.i.149).

The king and Polonius emerge from behind the tapestry. Claudius says that Hamlet's strange behavior has clearly not been caused by love for Ophelia and that his speech does not seem like the speech of insanity. He says that he fears that melancholy sits on something dangerous in Hamlet's soul like a bird sits on her egg, and that he fears what will happen when it hatches. He declares that he will send Hamlet to England, in the hope that a change of scenery might help him get over his troubles. Polonius agrees that this is a good idea, but he still believes that Hamlet's agitation comes from loving Ophelia. He asks Claudius to send Hamlet to Gertrude's chamber after the play, where Polonius can hide again and watch unseen; he hopes to learn whether Hamlet is really mad with love. Claudius agrees, saying that "[m]adness in great ones" must be carefully watched (III.i.187).

ANALYSIS

"To be, or not to be" is the most famous line in English literature. What does it mean? Why are these words and what follows special?

One reason is that they are a stunning example of Shakespeare's ability to make his characters seem three-dimensional. The audience senses that there is more to Hamlet's words than meets the ear—that there is something *behind* his words that is never spoken. Or, to put it another way, the audience witnesses signs of something within Hamlet's mind that even he isn't aware of. Hamlet is a fictional character who seems to possess a subconscious mind. How does Shakespeare manage to accomplish this?

In the first place, Hamlet doesn't talk directly about what he's really talking about. When he questions whether it is better "to be, or not to be," the obvious implication is, "Should I kill myself?" The entire soliloquy strongly suggests that he is toying with suicide and perhaps trying to work up his courage to do it. But at no point does he say that he is in pain or discuss why he *wants* to kill himself. In fact, he never says "I" or "me" in the entire speech. He's not trying to "express" himself at all; instead, he poses the question as a matter of philosophical debate. When he claims that everybody would commit suicide if they weren't uncertain about the afterlife, it sounds as if he's making an argument to convince an imaginary listener about an abstract point rather than directly addressing how the question applies to *him*. Now, it's perfectly ordinary for characters in plays to say something other than what they mean to other characters (this suggests that they are consciously hiding their true motives), but Hamlet does it when he's talking to himself. This creates the general impression that there are things going on in Hamlet's mind that he can't think about directly.

While we're on the subject of what's going on inside Hamlet's mind, consider his encounter with Ophelia. This conversation, closely watched by Claudius and Polonius, is, in fact, a test. It's supposed to establish whether Hamlet's madness stems from his lovesickness over Ophelia. Before we, the audience, see this encounter, we already think we know more than Claudius does: we know that Hamlet is only acting crazy, and that he's doing it to hide the fact that he's plotting against (or at least investigating) his uncle. Therefore, it *can't* be true that he's acting mad because of his love for Ophelia. But witnessing Hamlet's encounter with her throws everything we think we know into question.

Does Hamlet mean what he says to Ophelia? He says that he did love her once but that he doesn't love her now. There are several problems with concluding that Hamlet says the opposite of what he means in order to appear crazy. For one thing, if he really does love her, this is unnecessarily self-destructive behavior. It's unnecessary because it doesn't accomplish very much; that is, it doesn't make Claudius suspect him less. His professions of former love make him appear fickle, or emotionally withdrawn, rather than crazy.

Is Hamlet really crazy or just pretending? He announced ahead of time that he was going to act crazy, so it's hard to conclude that he (coincidentally) really went mad right after saying so. But his behavior toward Ophelia is both self-destructive and fraught with emotional intensity. It doesn't obviously further his plans. Moreover, his bitterness against Ophelia, and against women in general, resonates with his general discontentedness about the state of the world, the same discontentedness that he expresses when he thinks no one is watching. There is a passionate intensity to his unstable behavior that keeps us from viewing it as fake.

Perhaps it is worthwhile to ask this question: if a person in a rational state of mind decides to act as if he is crazy, to abuse the people around him regardless of whether he loves those people or hates them, and to give free expression to all of his most antisocial thoughts, when he starts to carry those actions out, will it even be possible to say at what point he stops pretending to be crazy and starts actually being crazy?

ACT III, SCENE II

SUMMARY

That evening, in the castle hall now doubling as a theater, Hamlet anxiously lectures the players on how to act the parts he has written for them. Polonius shuffles by with Rosencrantz and Guildenstern, and Hamlet dispatches them to hurry the players in their preparations. Horatio enters, and Hamlet, pleased to see him, praises him heartily, expressing his affection for and high opinion of Horatio's mind and manner, especially Horatio's qualities of self-control and reserve. Having told Horatio what he learned from the ghost—that Claudius murdered his father—he now asks him to watch Claudius carefully during the play so that they might compare their impressions of his behavior afterward. Horatio agrees, saying that if Claudius shows any signs of guilt, he will detect them.

The trumpets play a Danish march as the audience of lords and ladies begins streaming into the room. Hamlet warns Horatio that he will begin to act strangely. Sure enough, when Claudius asks how he is, his response seems quite insane: "Excellent, i' faith; of the chameleon's dish: I eat the air, promise-crammed" (III.ii.84–86). Hamlet asks Polonius about his history as an actor and torments Ophelia with a string of erotic puns.

The players enter and act out a brief, silent version of the play to come called a "dumbshow." In the dumbshow, a king and queen display their love. The queen leaves the king to sleep, and while he is sleeping, a man murders him by pouring poison into his ear. The murderer tries to seduce the queen, who gradually accepts his advances.

The players begin to enact the play in full, and we learn that the man who kills the king is the king's nephew. Throughout, Hamlet keeps up a running commentary on the characters and their actions, and continues to tease Ophelia with oblique sexual references.

When the murderer pours the poison into the sleeping king's ear, Claudius rises and cries out for light. Chaos ensues as the play comes to a sudden halt, the torches are lit, and the king flees the room, followed by the audience. When the scene quiets, Hamlet is left alone with Horatio.

Hamlet and Horatio agree that the king's behavior was telling. Now extremely excited, Hamlet continues to act frantic and scatter-brained, speaking glibly and inventing little poems. Rosencrantz and Guildenstern arrive to tell Hamlet that he is wanted in his mother's chambers. Rosencrantz asks again about the cause of Hamlet's "distemper," and Hamlet angrily accuses the pair of trying to play him as if he were a musical pipe. Polonius enters to escort Hamlet to the queen. Hamlet says he will go to her in a moment and asks for a moment alone. He steels himself to speak to his mother, resolving to be brutally honest with her but not to lose control of himself: "I will speak daggers to her, but use none" (III.ii.366).

ANALYSIS

In the first two scenes of Act III, Hamlet and Claudius both devise traps to catch one another's secrets: Claudius spies on Hamlet to discover the true nature of his madness, and Hamlet attempts to "catch the conscience of the king" in the theater (III.i.582). The play-within-a-play tells the story of Gonzago, the duke of Vienna, and his wife, Baptista, who marries his murdering nephew, Lucianus. Hamlet believes that the play is an opportunity to establish a more reliable basis for Claudius's guilt than the claims of the ghost. Since he has no way of knowing whether to believe a member of the spirit world, he tries to determine whether Claudius is guilty by reading his behavior for signs of a psychological state of guilt.

Although Hamlet exults at the success of his stratagem, interpreting Claudius's interruption isn't as simple as it seems. In the first place, Claudius does not react to the dumbshow, which exactly mimics the actions of which the ghost accuses Claudius. Claudius reacts to the play itself, which, unlike the dumbshow, makes it clear that *the king is murdered by his nephew.* Does Claudius react to being confronted with his own crimes, or to a play about uncle-killing sponsored by his crazy nephew? Or does he simply have indigestion?

Hamlet appears more in control of his own behavior in this scene than the one before, as shown by his effortless manipulations of

Rosencrantz and Guildenstern and his frank conversation with Horatio. He even expresses admiration and affection for Horatio's calm level-headedness, the lack of which is his own weakest point: "Give me that man / That is not passion's slave, and I will wear him / In my heart's core, ay, in my heart of heart, / As I do thee" (III.ii.64–67). In this scene he seems to prove that he is not insane after all, given the effortlessness with which he alternates between wild, erratic behavior and focused, sane behavior. He is excited but coherent during his conversation with Horatio before the play, but as soon as the king and queen enter, he begins to act insane, a sign that he is only pretending. His only questionable behavior in this scene arises in his crude comments to Ophelia, which show him capable of real cruelty. His misogyny has crossed rational bounds, and his every comment is laced with sexual innuendo. For instance, she comments, "You are keen, my lord, you are keen," complimenting him on his sharp intellect, and he replies, "It would cost you a groaning to take off my edge" (III.ii.227–228). His interchange with Ophelia is a mere prelude to the passionate rage he will unleash on Gertrude in the next scene.

ACT III, SCENE III

SUMMARY

Elsewhere in the castle, King Claudius speaks to Rosencrantz and Guildenstern. Badly shaken by the play and now considering Hamlet's madness to be dangerous, Claudius asks the pair to escort Hamlet on a voyage to England and to depart immediately. They agree and leave to make preparations. Polonius enters and reminds the king of his plan to hide in Gertrude's room and observe Hamlet's confrontation with her. He promises to tell Claudius all that he learns. When Polonius leaves, the king is alone, and he immediately expresses his guilt and grief over his sin. A brother's murder, he says, is the oldest sin and "hath the primal eldest curse upon't" (III.iii.37). He longs to ask for forgiveness, but says that he is unprepared to give up that which he gained by committing the murder, namely, the crown and the queen. He falls to his knees and begins to pray.

Hamlet slips quietly into the room and steels himself to kill the unseeing Claudius. But suddenly it occurs to him that if he kills Claudius while he is praying, he will end the king's life at the moment when he was seeking forgiveness for his sins, sending Claudius's soul to heaven. This is hardly an adequate revenge, Hamlet thinks, especially since Claudius, by killing Hamlet's father before he had time to make his last confession, ensured that his brother would not go to heaven. Hamlet decides to wait, resolving to kill Claudius when the king is sinning—when he is either drunk, angry, or lustful. He leaves. Claudius rises and declares that he has been unable to pray sincerely: "My words fly up, my thoughts remain below" (III.iii.96).

ANALYSIS

> *Thus conscience does make cowards of us all;*
> *And thus the native hue of resolution*
> *Is sicklied o'er with the pale cast of thought;*
> *And enterprises of great pith and moment,*
> *With this regard, their currents turn awry,*
> *And lose the name of action.*
>
> (III.i.85–90)
>
> (See QUOTATIONS, p. 66)

In Act III, scene iii, Hamlet finally seems ready to put his desire for revenge into action. He is satisfied that the play has proven his uncle's guilt. When Claudius prays, the audience is given real certainty that Claudius murdered his brother: a full, spontaneous confession, even though nobody else hears it. This only heightens our sense that the climax of the play is due to arrive. But Hamlet waits.

On the surface, it seems that he waits because he wants a more radical revenge. Critics such as Samuel Taylor Coleridge have been horrified by Hamlet's words here—he completely oversteps the bounds of Christian morality in trying to damn his opponent's soul as well as kill him. But apart from this ultraviolent posturing, Hamlet has once again avoided the imperative to act by involving himself in a problem of knowledge. Now that he's satisfied that he knows Claudius's guilt, he wants to know that his punishment will be sufficient. It may have been difficult to prove the former, but how can Hamlet ever hope to know the fate of Claudius's immortal soul?

Hamlet poses his desire to damn Claudius as a matter of fairness: his own father was killed without having cleansed his soul by praying or confessing, so why should his murderer be given that chance? But Hamlet is forced to admit that he doesn't really know what happened to his father, remarking "how his audit stands, who knows, save heaven?" (III.iv.82). The most he can say is that "in our circumstance and course of thought / 'Tis heavy with him" (III.iv.83–84). *The Norton Shakespeare* paraphrases "in our circumstance and course of thought" as "in our indirect and limited way of knowing on earth." Having proven his uncle's guilt to himself, against all odds, Hamlet suddenly finds something else to be uncertain about.

At this point, Hamlet has gone beyond his earlier need to know the facts about the crime, and he now craves metaphysical knowledge, knowledge of the afterlife and of God, before he is willing to act. The audience has had plenty of opportunity to see that Hamlet is fascinated with philosophical questions. In the case of the "to be, or not to be" soliloquy, we saw that his philosophizing can be a way for him to avoid thinking about or acknowledging something more immediately important (in that case, his urge to kill himself). Is Hamlet using his speculations about Claudius's soul to avoid thinking about something in this case? Perhaps the task he has set for himself—killing another human being in cold blood—is too much for him to face. Whatever it is, the audience may once again get the sense that there is something more to Hamlet's behavior than meets the eye. That Shakespeare is able to convey this sense is a remarkable achievement in itself, quite apart from how we try to explain what Hamlet's unacknowledged motives might be.

ACT III, SCENE IV

SUMMARY

In Gertrude's chamber, the queen and Polonius wait for Hamlet's arrival. Polonius plans to hide in order to eavesdrop on Gertrude's confrontation with her son, in the hope that doing so will enable him to determine the cause of Hamlet's bizarre and threatening behavior. Polonius urges the queen to be harsh with Hamlet when he arrives, saying that she should chastise him for his recent behavior. Gertrude agrees, and Polonius hides behind an arras, or tapestry.

Hamlet storms into the room and asks his mother why she has sent for him. She says that he has offended his father, meaning his stepfather, Claudius. He interrupts her and says that she has offended his father, meaning the dead King Hamlet, by marrying

Claudius. Hamlet accosts her with an almost violent intensity and declares his intention to make her fully aware of the profundity of her sin. Fearing for her life, Gertrude cries out. From behind the arras, Polonius calls out for help. Hamlet, realizing that someone is behind the arras and suspecting that it might be Claudius, cries, "How now! a rat?" (III.iv.22). He draws his sword and stabs it through the tapestry, killing the unseen Polonius. Gertrude asks what Hamlet has done, and he replies, "Nay, I know not: / Is it the king?" (III.iv.24). The queen says his action was a "rash and bloody" deed, and Hamlet replies that it was almost as rash and bloody as murdering a king and marrying his brother (III.iv.26–28). Disbelieving, the queen exclaims, "As kill a king!" and Hamlet replies that she heard him correctly (III.iv.29).

Hamlet lifts the arras and discovers Polonius's body: he has not killed the king and achieved his revenge but has murdered the relatively innocent Polonius. He bids the old man farewell, calling him an "intruding fool" (III.iv.30). He turns to his mother, declaring that he will wring her heart. He shows her a picture of the dead king and a picture of the current king, bitterly comments on the superiority of his father to his uncle, and asks her furiously what has driven her to marry a rotten man such as Claudius. She pleads with him to stop, saying that he has turned her eyes onto her soul and that she does not like what she sees there. Hamlet continues to denounce her and rail against Claudius, until, suddenly, the ghost of his father again appears before him.

Hamlet speaks to the apparition, but Gertrude is unable to see it and believes him to be mad. The ghost intones that it has come to remind Hamlet of his purpose, that Hamlet has not yet killed Claudius and must achieve his revenge. Noting that Gertrude is amazed and unable to see him, the ghost asks Hamlet to intercede with her. Hamlet describes the ghost, but Gertrude sees nothing, and in a moment the ghost disappears. Hamlet tries desperately to convince Gertrude that he is not mad but has merely feigned madness all along, and he urges her to forsake Claudius and regain her good conscience. He urges her as well not to reveal to Claudius that his madness has been an act. Gertrude, still shaken from Hamlet's furious condemnation of her, agrees to keep his secret. He bids her goodnight, but, before he leaves, he points to Polonius's corpse and declares that heaven has "punished me with this, and this with me" (III.iv.158). Hamlet reminds his mother that he must sail to England with Rosencrantz and Guildenstern, whom he says he will regard with suspicion, as though they were poisonous snakes, since he assumes that their loyalties are with Claudius, not with him. Dragging Polonius's body behind him, Hamlet leaves his mother's room.

ANALYSIS

What is Hamlet trying to do in his confrontation with his mother? It is possible that he wants her to confirm her knowledge of Claudius's crime, to provide further proof of his guilt. Or it may be that Hamlet wants to know whether she was complicit in the crime. Or he may feel that he needs her on his side if he is to achieve justice. While all of these are possibilities, what Hamlet actually does is urge his mother to repent choosing Claudius over his own father. More specifically, he repeatedly demands that she avoid Claudius's bed. Actually, he's much more specific: he tells her not to let Claudius arouse her by fondling her neck, not to stay within his semen-infested sheets, and other shockingly graphic details.

This is another point in the play where audiences and readers have felt that there is more going on in Hamlet's brain than we can quite put our fingers on. Sigmund Freud wrote that Hamlet harbors an unconscious desire to sexually enjoy his mother. Freud maintained that all men unconsciously desire their mothers in this way, and he called this the "Oedipus Complex," after the character in Sophocles' play who unwittingly murders his father and has several children by his own mother. Whether or not Freud was right about this is as difficult to prove as any of the problems that Hamlet worries about, but his argument in regard to Hamlet is quite remarkable. He says that while Oedipus actually enacts this fantasy, Hamlet only betrays the unconscious desire to do so. Hamlet is thus a quintessentially modern person, because he has repressed desires.

Though Gertrude's speech in this scene is largely limited to brief reactions to Hamlet's lengthy denunciations of her, it is our most revealing look at her character. As the scene progresses, Gertrude goes through several states of feeling: she is haughty and accusatory at the beginning, then afraid that Hamlet will hurt her, shocked and upset when Hamlet kills Polonius, overwhelmed by fear and panic as Hamlet accosts her, and disbelieving when Hamlet sees the ghost. Finally, she is contrite toward her son and apparently willing to take his part and help him. For Gertrude, then, the scene progresses as a sequence of great shocks, each of which weakens her resistance to Hamlet's condemnation of her behavior. Of course, Gertrude is convinced mainly by Hamlet's insistence and power of feeling, illustrating what many readers have felt to be her central characteristic: her tendency to be dominated by powerful men and her need for men to show her what to think and how to feel.

This quality explains why Gertrude would have turned to Claudius so soon after her husband's death, and it also explains why she so quickly adopts Hamlet's point of view in this scene. Of course, the play does not specifically explain Gertrude's behavior. It is possible that she was complicit with Claudius in the murder of her husband, though that seems unlikely given her surprised reaction to Hamlet's accusation in this scene, and it is possible that she merely pretends to take Hamlet's side to placate him, which would explain why she immediately reports his behavior to Claudius after promising not to do so. But another interpretation of Gertrude's character seems to be that she has a powerful instinct for self-preservation and advancement that leads her to rely too deeply on men. Not only does this interpretation explain her behavior throughout much of the play; it also links her thematically to Ophelia, the play's other important female character, who is also submissive and utterly dependent on men.

Hamlet's rash, murderous action in stabbing Polonius is an important illustration of his inability to coordinate his thoughts and actions, which might be considered his tragic flaw. In his passive, thoughtful mode, Hamlet is too beset by moral considerations and uncertainties to avenge his father's death by killing Claudius, even when the opportunity is before him. But when he does choose to act, he does so blindly, stabbing his anonymous "enemy" through a curtain. It is as if Hamlet is so distrustful of the possibility of acting rationally that he believes his revenge is more likely to come about as an accident than as a premeditated act.

When he sees Polonius's corpse, Hamlet interprets his misdeed within the terms of retribution, punishment, and vengeance: "Heaven hath pleased it so / To punish me with this, and this with me" (III.iv.157–158). Though Hamlet has not achieved his vengeance upon Claudius, he believes that God has used him as a tool of vengeance to punish Polonius's sins and punish Hamlet's sins by staining his soul with the murder.

ACT IV, SCENES I–II

SUMMARY: ACT IV, SCENE I

Frantic after her confrontation with Hamlet, Gertrude hurries to Claudius, who is conferring with Rosencrantz and Guildenstern. She asks to speak to the king alone. When Rosencrantz and Guildenstern exit, she tells Claudius about her encounter with Hamlet. She says that he is as mad as the sea during a violent storm; she also tells Claudius that Hamlet has killed Polonius. Aghast, the king notes that had he been concealed behind the arras, Hamlet would have killed him. Claudius wonders aloud how he will be able to handle this public crisis without damaging his hold on Denmark. He tells Gertrude that they must ship Hamlet to England at once and find a way to explain Hamlet's misdeed to the court and to the people. He calls Rosencrantz and Guildenstern, tells them about the murder, and sends them to find Hamlet.

SUMMARY: ACT IV, SCENE II

Elsewhere in Elsinore, Hamlet has just finished disposing of Polonius's body, commenting that the corpse has been "safely stowed" (IV.ii.1). Rosencrantz and Guildenstern appear and ask what he has done with the body. Hamlet refuses to give them a straight answer, instead saying, "The body is with the king, but the king is not with the body" (IV.ii.25–26). Feigning offense at being questioned, he accuses them of being spies in the service of Claudius. He calls Rosencrantz a "sponge . . . that soaks up the king's countenance, his rewards, his authorities," and warns him that "when he needs what you have gleaned, it is but squeezing you, and, sponge, you shall be dry again" (IV.ii.11–19). At last he agrees to allow Rosencrantz and Guildenstern to escort him to Claudius.

ANALYSIS: ACT IV, SCENES I–II

The short first scene of Act IV centers around Gertrude's betrayal of her son, turning him in to the king after having promised to help him. While she does keep her promise not to reveal that Hamlet was only pretending to be insane, the immediate and frank way in which she tells Claudius about Hamlet's behavior and his murder of Polonius implies that she sees herself as allied to the king rather than to her son. Whether Gertrude really believes Hamlet to be mad, or has simply recognized that her best interest lies in allying herself with Claudius regardless of what she believes, is impossible to determine from this scene and is largely a matter of one's personal interpretation of the events. Whatever the case, it is Gertrude's speech to Claudius that cements the king's secret plan to have Hamlet executed in England.

As brief as it is, Act IV, scene i is a magnificent example of Shakespeare's skill at developing characters, illustrated by the subtle development of Claudius. Where most of the other male characters in the play, including Hamlet, King Hamlet, Laertes, and Fortinbras, are obsessed with themes of honor, moral balance, and retributive justice, Claudius is a selfish, ambitious king who is more concerned with maintaining his own power and averting political danger than achieving justice through his rule. His response to Gertrude's revelation that Hamlet has killed Polonius is extremely telling. Rather than considering that Gertrude might have been in danger, he immediately remarks that had he been in the room, *he* would have been in danger. Hamlet must be sent away from Denmark, he thinks, not as punishment for committing murder but because he represents a danger to Claudius. And as soon as he hears of the murder, Claudius's mind begins working to find a way to characterize the killing so that it does not seem like a political crisis to his court and to the people of Denmark. To do this, he says, will require all his "majesty and skill" (IV.i.30). In this scene and the scenes to follow, Shakespeare creates in Claudius a convincing depiction of a conniving, ambitious politician. In this way, Claudius emerges as a figure of powerful contrast to the more forthright men in the play, including Laertes, Fortinbras, and Horatio, and the far more morally conscious Prince Hamlet.

Hamlet's murder of Polonius at the end of Act III is one of the most disturbing moments in the play. If it was previously possible to consider Hamlet a "hero" or an idealized version of a human being, it is no longer possible after he kills Polonius. His sensitive, reflective nature—the trait that constantly interfered with his ability to take revenge on Claudius—now disappears in the wake of its violent opposite: a rash, murderous explosion of activity. Hamlet leaps to the conclusion that Claudius is behind the arras, or else he simply lashes out thoughtlessly. In any case, Hamlet's moral superiority to Claudius is now thrown into question. He has killed Polonius just as Claudius killed Hamlet's father, the only differences being that Hamlet's murder was not premeditated and was not committed out of jealousy or ambition. Hamlet also eases his conscience with the fact that Polonius was dishonestly spying on Hamlet at the moment when he was killed. But the result of Hamlet's deed is very similar to that of Claudius's: Laertes and Ophelia have lost a father, just as Hamlet himself did.

Now, Hamlet hides the body. But rather than being overwhelmed with contrition, as we might expect of a hero who has committed such a terrible mistake, he seems manic, desperate, and self-righteous, especially in his condemnation of Rosencrantz and Guildenstern. Throughout Act IV, scene ii, as in the play-within-a-play scene (Act III, scene ii), Hamlet's biting, ironic wit is combined with his rash, impulsive streak, and his feigned madness seems very close to the real thing. Though Hamlet has many admirable qualities, scenes such as this one serve as powerful reminders that we are not meant to take the prince as an unqualified hero.

ACT IV, SCENES III–IV

SUMMARY: ACT IV, SCENE III
The king speaks to a group of attendants, telling them of Polonius's death and his intention to send Hamlet to England. Rosencrantz and Guildenstern appear with Hamlet, who is under guard. Pressed by Claudius to reveal the location of Polonius's body, Hamlet is by turns inane, coy, and clever, saying that Polonius is being eaten by worms, and that the king could send a messenger to find Polonius in heaven or seek him in hell himself. Finally, Hamlet reveals that Polonius's body is under the stairs near the castle lobby, and the king dispatches his attendants to look there. The king tells Hamlet that he must leave at once for England, and Hamlet enthusiastically agrees. He exits, and Claudius sends Rosencrantz and Guildenstern to ensure that he boards the ship at once. Alone with his thoughts, Claudius states his hope that England will obey the sealed orders he has sent with Rosencrantz and Guildenstern. The orders call for Prince Hamlet to be put to death.

SUMMARY: ACT IV, SCENE IV
On a nearby plain in Denmark, young Prince Fortinbras marches at the head of his army, traveling through Denmark on the way to attack Poland. Fortinbras orders his captain to go and ask the king of Denmark for permission to travel through his lands. On his way, the captain encounters Hamlet, Rosencrantz, and Guildenstern on

their way to the ship bound for England. The captain informs them that the Norwegian army rides to fight the Poles. Hamlet asks about the basis of the conflict, and the man tells him that the armies will fight over "a little patch of land / That hath in it no profit but the name" (IV.iv.98–99). Astonished by the thought that a bloody war could be fought over something so insignificant, Hamlet marvels that human beings are able to act so violently and purposefully for so little gain. By comparison, Hamlet has a great deal to gain from seeking his own bloody revenge on Claudius, and yet he still delays and fails to act toward his purpose. Disgusted with himself for having failed to gain his revenge on Claudius, Hamlet declares that from this moment on, his thoughts will be bloody.

Analysis: Act IV, scenes iii–iv

As we saw in Act IV, scene ii, the murder of Polonius and the subsequent traumatic encounter with his mother seem to leave Hamlet in a frantic, unstable frame of mind, the mode in which his excitable nature seems very similar to actual madness. He taunts Claudius, toward whom his hostility is now barely disguised, and makes light of Polonius's murder with word games. He also pretends to be thrilled at the idea of sailing for England with Rosencrantz and Guildenstern.

On some level he is prepared for what is to come. His farewell to his mother proved as much, when he told her that he would trust his old schoolfellows as if they were "adders fang'd," that is, poisonous snakes (III.iv.185.2). But although Hamlet suspects his friends' treachery, he may not fully realize the malevolence of Claudius's designs for him. Claudius's subterfuge in asking the English to execute Hamlet reveals the extent to which he now fears Hamlet: whether Hamlet is sane or mad, he is a danger to Claudius, and Claudius wishes him to die. It is also revealing that one of Claudius's considerations in seeking to have Hamlet murdered in far-off England, rather than merely executing him in Denmark, is that he is beloved by the common people of Denmark—"loved of the distracted multitude," as Claudius says (IV.iii.4). Again, where King Hamlet was a brave warrior, King Claudius is a crafty politician, constantly working to strengthen his own power, circumvent threats to his throne, and manipulate those around him to his own advantage.

Act IV, scene iv restores the focus of the play to the theme of human action. Hamlet's encounter with the Norwegian captain serves to remind the reader of Fortinbras's presence in the world of the play and gives Hamlet another example of the will to action that he lacks. Earlier, he was amazed by the player's evocation of powerful feeling for Hecuba, a legendary character who meant nothing to him (II.ii). Now, he is awestruck by the willingness of Fortinbras to devote the energy of an entire army, probably wasting hundreds of lives and risking his own, to reclaim a worthless scrap of land in Poland. Hamlet considers the moral ambiguity of Fortinbras's action, but more than anything else he is impressed by the forcefulness of it, and that forcefulness becomes a kind of ideal toward which Hamlet decides at last to strive. "My thoughts be bloody, or be nothing worth!" he declares (IV.iv.9.56). Of course, he fails to put this exclamation into action, as he has failed at every previous turn to achieve his revenge on Claudius. "My *thoughts* be bloody," Hamlet says. Tellingly, he does not say "My *deeds* be bloody."

ACT IV, SCENES V–VI

SUMMARY: ACT IV, SCENE V

Gertrude and Horatio discuss Ophelia. Gertrude does not wish to see the bereaved girl, but Horatio says that Ophelia should be pitied, explaining that her grief has made her disordered and incoherent. Ophelia enters. Adorned with flowers and singing strange songs, she seems to have gone mad. Claudius enters and hears Ophelia's ravings, such as, "They say the owl was a baker's daughter" (IV.v.42). He says that Ophelia's grief stems from her father's death, and that the people have been suspicious and disturbed by the death as well: "muddied, / Thick and unwholesome in their thoughts and whispers / For good Polonius' death" (IV.v.77–79). He also mentions that Laertes has secretly sailed back from France.

A loud noise echoes from somewhere in the castle. Claudius calls for his guards, and a gentleman enters to warn the king that Laertes has come with a mob of commoners. The mob calls Laertes "lord," according to the gentlemen, and the people whisper that "Laertes shall be king" (IV.v.102–106). A furious Laertes storms into the hall, fuming in his desire to avenge his father's death. Claudius attempts to soothe him by frankly acknowledging that Polonius is dead. Gertrude nervously adds that Claudius is innocent in it. When Ophelia reenters, obviously insane, Laertes plunges again into rage. Claudius claims that he is not responsible for Polonius's death and says that Laertes' desire for revenge is a credit to him, so long as he seeks revenge upon the proper person. Claudius convinces Laertes to hear his version of events, which he says will answer all his questions. Laertes agrees, and Claudius seconds his desire to achieve justice in the aftermath of Polonius's death: "Where th' offence is, let the great axe fall" (IV.v.213).

SUMMARY: ACT IV, SCENE VI
In another part of the castle, Horatio is introduced to a pair of sailors bearing a letter for him from Hamlet. In the letter, Hamlet says that his ship was captured by pirates, who have returned him to Denmark. He asks Horatio to escort the sailors to the king and queen, for they have messages for them as well. He also says that he has much to tell of Rosencrantz and Guildenstern. Horatio takes the sailors to the king and then follows them to find Hamlet, who is in the countryside near the castle.

ANALYSIS: ACT IV, SCENES V–VI
As we have seen, one of the important themes of *Hamlet* is the connection between the health of a state and the moral legitimacy of its ruler. Claudius is rotten, and, as a result, Denmark is rotten, too. Here, at the beginning of Act IV, scene v, things have palpably darkened for the nation: Hamlet is gone, Polonius is dead and has been buried in secret, Ophelia is raving mad, and, as Claudius tells us, the common people are disturbed and murmuring among themselves. This ominous turn of events leads to the truncated, miniature rebellion that accompanies Laertes' return to Denmark. Acting as the wronged son operating with open fury, Laertes has all the moral legitimacy that Claudius lacks, the legitimacy that Hamlet has forfeited through his murder of Polonius and his delay in avenging his father's death.

Laertes is Hamlet's best foil throughout the play, and in this scene the contrast between the two, each of whom has a dead father to avenge, reaches its peak. (A third figure with a dead father to avenge, Fortinbras, lurks on the horizon.) Whereas Hamlet is reflective and has difficulty acting, Laertes is active and has no use for thought. He has no interest in moral concerns, only in his consuming desire to avenge Polonius. When Claudius later asks Laertes how far he would go to avenge his father, Laertes replies that he would slit Hamlet's throat in the church (IV.vii.98). This statement, indicating his willingness to murder Hamlet even in a sacred place of worship, brings into sharp relief the contrast between the two sons: recall that Hamlet declined to kill Claudius as the king knelt in prayer (III.iii).

As befits a scene full of anger and dark thoughts, Act IV, scene v brings a repetition of the motif of insanity, this time through the character of Ophelia, who has truly been driven mad by the death of her father. Shakespeare has demonstrated Ophelia's chaste dependence on the men in her life; after Polonius's sudden death and Hamlet's subsequent exile, she finds herself abruptly without any of them. Ophelia's lunatic ravings reveal a great deal about the nature of her mind at this stage in her young life. She is obsessed with death, beauty, and an ambiguous sexual desire, expressed in startlingly frank imagery:

> Young men will do't, if they come to't,
> By Cock, they are to blame.
> Quoth she
> 'Before you tumbled me,
> You promised me to wed.'
>
> (IV.v.59–62)

Some readers have interpreted passages such as these, combined with Hamlet's sexually explicit taunting of Ophelia in Act III, scene ii, as evidence that Ophelia's relationship with Hamlet was sexual in nature. Of course, this is impossible to conclude with any certainty, but from these lines it is apparent that Ophelia is grappling with sexuality and that her sexual feelings, discouraged by her father, her brother, and her society, are close to the forefront of her mind as she slips into insanity. But, most important, Ophelia's insanity is designed to contrast strongly with Hamlet's, differing primarily in its legitimacy: Ophelia does not feign madness to achieve an end, but is truly driven mad by external pressures. Many of the worst elements in Denmark, including madness, fear, and rebellion, so far have been kept hidden under various disguises, such as Hamlet's pretense and Claudius's court revelry, and are now beginning to emerge into the open.

After exiling Hamlet to England in Act IV, scene iv, Shakespeare now returns him to Denmark only two scenes later through the bizarre deus ex machina—an improbable or unexpected device or character introduced to resolve a situation in a work of fiction or drama—of the pirate attack. The short Act IV, scene vi is primarily devoted to plot development, as Horatio reads Hamlet's letter narrating his adventure. The story of the pirate attack has little to do with the main themes of the play, but it does provide an interesting variation on the idea of retributive justice, since instead of punishing someone for doing something wrong, Hamlet states his intention to reward the pirates for the right they have done in returning him to Denmark. "They have dealt with me like thieves of mercy," he says, "but they knew what they did: I am to do a good turn for them" (IV.vi.17–19). Additionally, Hamlet's letter features a return of the motif of ears and hearing, as the prince tells Horatio that "I have words to speak in thine ear will make thee dumb," an open reference to the poison poured into King Hamlet's ear by the murderous Claudius (IV.vi.21).

ACT IV, SCENE VII

SUMMARY

As Horatio speaks to the sailors, Claudius and a calmer Laertes discuss Polonius's death. Claudius explains that he acted as he did, burying Polonius secretly and not punishing Hamlet for the murder, because both the common people and the queen love Hamlet very much. As a king and as a husband, he did not wish to upset either of them. A messenger enters with the letter from Hamlet to Claudius, which informs the king that Hamlet will return tomorrow. Laertes is pleased that Hamlet has come back to Denmark, since it means that his revenge will not be delayed.

Claudius agrees that Laertes deserves to be revenged upon Hamlet, and he is disposed to encourage Laertes to kill Hamlet, since Hamlet's erratic behavior has made him a threat to Claudius's reign. The devious king begins to think of a way for Laertes to ensure his revenge without creating any appearance of foul play. He recalls that Hamlet has been jealous in the past of Laertes' prowess with a sword, which was recently praised before all the court by a Frenchman who had seen him in combat. The king speculates that if Hamlet could be tempted into a duel with Laertes, it might provide Laertes with the chance to kill him. Laertes agrees, and they settle on a plan. Laertes will use a sharpened sword rather than the customary dull fencing blade. Laertes also proposes to poison his sword, so that even a scratch from it will kill Hamlet.

The king concocts a backup plan as well, proposing that if Hamlet succeeds in the duel, Claudius will offer him a poisoned cup of wine to drink from in celebration.

Gertrude enters with tragic news. Ophelia, mad with grief, has drowned in the river. Anguished to have lost his sister so soon after his father's death, Laertes flees the room. Claudius summons Gertrude to follow. He tells her it was nearly impossible to quiet Laertes' rage, and worries that the news of Ophelia's death will reawaken it.

ANALYSIS

The scheming Claudius encounters Laertes at approximately the same moment as he learns that Hamlet has survived and returned to Denmark. Claudius's behavior throughout this scene, as in Act IV, scene v, shows him at his most devious and calculating. Shakespeare shows Claudius's mind working overtime to derail Laertes' anger, which is thus far the greatest challenge his kingship has faced. In Act IV, scene v, Claudius decided that the way to appease Laertes was by appearing frank and honest. When Laertes asked furiously where his father was, Claudius replied, "Dead" (IV.v.123). Additionally, in a masterful stroke of characterization, Shakespeare has the nervous Gertrude, unable to see Claudius's plan, follow this statement with a quick insistence on Claudius's innocence: "But not by him" (IV.v.123).

In this scene, Claudius has clearly decided that he can appease Laertes' wrath and dispense with Hamlet in a single stroke: he hits upon the idea of the duel in order to use Laertes' rage to ensure Hamlet's death. The resulting plan brings both the theme of revenge and the repeated use of traps in the plot to a new height—Laertes and Claudius concoct not one but three covert mechanisms by which Hamlet may be killed.

Ophelia's tragic death occurs at the worst possible moment for Claudius. As Laertes flees the room in agony, Claudius follows, not to console or even to join him in mourning but because, as he tells Gertrude, it was so difficult to appease his anger in the first place. Claudius does not have time to worry about the victims of tragedy—he is too busy dealing with threats to his own power.

The image of Ophelia drowning amid her garlands of flowers has proved to be one of the most enduring images in the play, represented countless times by artists and poets throughout the centuries. Ophelia is associated with flower imagery from the beginning of the play. In her first scene, Polonius presents her with a violet; after she goes mad, she sings songs about flowers; and now she drowns amid long streams of them. The fragile beauty of the flowers resembles Ophelia's own fragile beauty, as well as her nascent sexuality and her exquisite, doomed innocence.

ACT V, SCENE I

SUMMARY

In the churchyard, two gravediggers shovel out a grave for Ophelia. They argue whether Ophelia should be buried in the churchyard, since her death looks like a suicide. According to religious doctrine, suicides may not receive Christian burial. The first gravedigger, who speaks cleverly and mischievously, asks the second gravedigger a riddle: "What is he that builds stronger than either the mason, the shipwright, or the carpenter?" (V.i.46–47). The second gravedigger answers that it must be the gallows-maker, for his frame outlasts a thousand tenants. The first gravedigger corrects him, saying that it is the gravedigger, for his "houses" will last until Doomsday.

Hamlet and Horatio enter at a distance and watch the gravediggers work. Hamlet looks with wonder at the skulls they excavate to make room for the fresh grave and speculates darkly about what occupations the owners of these skulls served in life: "Why may not that be the skull of a lawyer? Where be his quiddities now . . . ?" (V.i.90–91). Hamlet asks the gravedigger whose grave he digs, and the gravedigger spars with him verbally, first claiming that the grave is his own, since he is digging it, then that the grave belongs to no man and no woman, because men and women are living things and the occupant of the grave will be dead. At last he admits that it belongs to one "that was a woman sir; but, rest her soul, she's dead" (V.i.146). The gravedigger, who does not recognize Hamlet as the prince, tells him that he has been a gravedigger since King Hamlet defeated the elder Fortinbras in battle, the very day on which young Prince Hamlet was born. Hamlet picks up a skull, and the gravedigger tells him that the skull belonged to Yorick, King Hamlet's jester. Hamlet tells Horatio that as a child he knew Yorick and is appalled at the sight of the skull. He realizes forcefully that all men will eventually become dust, even great men like Alexander the Great and Julius Caesar. Hamlet imagines that Julius Caesar has disintegrated and is now part of the dust used to patch up a wall.

SUMMARY & ANALYSIS

Suddenly, the funeral procession for Ophelia enters the church-yard, including Claudius, Gertrude, Laertes, and many mourning courtiers. Hamlet, wondering who has died, notices that the funeral rites seem "maimed," indicating that the dead man or woman took his or her own life (V.i.242). He and Horatio hide as the procession approaches the grave. As Ophelia is laid in the earth, Hamlet real-izes it is she who has died. At the same moment, Laertes becomes infuriated with the priest, who says that to give Ophelia a proper Christian burial would profane the dead. Laertes leaps into Ophelia's grave to hold her once again in his arms. Grief-stricken and outraged, Hamlet bursts upon the company, declaring in ago-nized fury his own love for Ophelia. He leaps into the grave and fights with Laertes, saying that "forty thousand brothers / Could not, with all their quantity of love, / make up my sum" (V.i.254–256). Hamlet cries that he would do things for Ophelia that Laertes could not dream of—he would eat a crocodile for her, he would be buried alive with her. The combatants are pulled apart by the funeral company. Gertrude and Claudius declare that Hamlet is mad. Hamlet storms off, and Horatio follows. The king urges Laertes to be patient, and to remember their plan for revenge.

ANALYSIS

The gravediggers are designated as "clowns" in the stage directions and prompts, and it is important to note that in Shakespeare's time the word clown referred to a rustic or peasant, and did not mean that the person in question was funny or wore a costume.

The gravediggers represent a humorous type commonly found in Shakespeare's plays: the clever commoner who gets the better of his social superior through wit. At the Globe Theater, this type of char-acter may have particularly appealed to the "groundlings," the mem-bers of the audience who could not afford seats and thus stood on the ground. Though they are usually figures of merriment, in this scene the gravediggers assume a rather macabre tone, since their jests and jibes are all made in a cemetery, among bones of the dead. Their con-versation about Ophelia, however, furthers an important theme in the play: the question of the moral legitimacy of suicide under theo-logical law. By giving this serious subject a darkly comic interpreta-tion, Shakespeare essentially makes a grotesque parody of Hamlet's earlier "To be, or not to be" soliloquy (III.i), indicating the collapse of every lasting value in the play into uncertainty and absurdity.

Hamlet's confrontation with death, manifested primarily in his discovery of Yorick's skull, is, like Ophelia's drowning, an enduring image from the play. However, his solemn theorizing explodes in grief and rage when he sees Ophelia's funeral procession, and his assault on Laertes offers a glimpse of what his true feelings for Ophelia might once have been. Laertes' passionate embrace of the dead Ophelia again advances the subtle motif of incest that hangs over their brother-sister relationship. Interestingly, Hamlet never expresses a sense of guilt over Ophelia's death, which he indirectly caused through his murder of Polonius. In fact, the only time he even comes close to taking responsibility for Polonius's death at all comes in the next and last scene, when he apologizes to Laertes before the duel, blaming his "madness" for Polonius's death. This seems wholly inadequate, given that Hamlet has previously claimed repeatedly only to be feigning madness. But by the same token, to expect moral completeness from a character as troubled as Hamlet might be unrealistic. After all, Hamlet's defining characteristics are his pain, his fear, and his self-conflict. Were he to take full responsibility for the consequences of Polonius's death, he would probably not be able to withstand the psychological torment of the resulting guilt.

A notable minor motif that is developed in this scene is Hamlet's obsession with the physicality of death. Though many of his thoughts about death concern the spiritual consequences of dying— for instance, torment in the afterlife—he is nearly as fascinated by the physical decomposition of the body. This is nowhere more evident than in his preoccupation with Yorick's skull, when he envisions physical features such as lips and skin that have decomposed from the bone. Recall that Hamlet previously commented to Claudius that Polonius's body was at supper, because it was being eaten by worms (IV.iii). He is also fascinated by the equalizing effect of death and decomposition: great men and beggars both end as dust. In this scene, he imagines dust from the decomposed corpse of Julius Caesar being used to patch a wall; earlier, in Act IV, he noted, "A man may fish with the worm that have eat of a king, and eat of the fish that hath fed of that worm," a metaphor by which he illustrates "how a king may go a progress through the guts of a beggar" (IV.iii.26–31).

ACT V, SCENE II

SUMMARY

The next day at Elsinore Castle, Hamlet tells Horatio how he plotted to overcome Claudius's scheme to have him murdered in England. He replaced the sealed letter carried by the unsuspecting Rosencrantz and Guildenstern, which called for Hamlet's execution, with one calling for the execution of the bearers of the letter—Rosencrantz and Guildenstern themselves. He tells Horatio that he has no sympathy for Rosencrantz and Guildenstern, who betrayed him and catered to Claudius, but that he feels sorry for having behaved with such hostility toward Laertes. In Laertes' desire to avenge his father's death, he says, he sees the mirror image of his own desire, and he promises to seek Laertes' good favor.

Their conversation is interrupted by Osric, a foolish courtier. Osric tries to flatter Hamlet by agreeing with everything Hamlet says, even when he contradicts himself; in the space of seconds, he agrees first that it is cold, then that it is hot. He has come to tell them that Claudius wants Hamlet to fence with Laertes and that the king has made a wager with Laertes that Hamlet will win. Then Osric begins to praise Laertes effusively, though Hamlet and Horatio are unable to determine what point he is trying to make with his overly elaborate proclamations. Finally, a lord enters and asks Hamlet if he is ready to come to the match, as the king and queen are expecting him. Against Horatio's advice, Hamlet agrees to fight, saying that "all's ill here about my heart," but that one must be ready for death, since it will come no matter what one does (V.ii.222). The court marches into the hall, and Hamlet asks Laertes for forgiveness, claiming that it was his madness, and not his own will, that murdered Polonius. Laertes says that he will not forgive Hamlet until an elder, an expert in the fine points of honor, has advised him in the matter. But, in the meantime, he says, he will accept Hamlet's offer of love.

They select their foils (blunted swords used in fencing), and the king says that if Hamlet wins the first or second hit, he will drink to Hamlet's health, then throw into the cup a valuable gem (actually the poison) and give the wine to Hamlet. The duel begins. Hamlet strikes Laertes but declines to drink from the cup, saying that he will play another hit first. He hits Laertes again, and Gertrude rises to drink from the cup. The king tells her not to drink, but she does so anyway. In an aside, Claudius murmurs, "It is the poison'd cup: it is too late" (V.ii.235). Laertes remarks under his breath that to wound Hamlet with the poisoned sword is almost against his conscience. But they fight again, and Laertes scores a hit against Hamlet, drawing blood. Scuffling, they manage to exchange swords, and Hamlet wounds Laertes with Laertes' own blade.

The queen falls. Laertes, poisoned by his own sword, declares, "I am justly kill'd with my own treachery" (V.ii.318). The queen moans that the cup must have been poisoned, calls out to Hamlet, and dies. Laertes tells Hamlet that he, too, has been slain, by his own poisoned sword, and that the king is to blame both for the poison on the sword and for the poison in the cup. Hamlet, in a fury, runs Claudius through with the poisoned sword and forces him to drink down the rest of the poisoned wine. Claudius dies crying out for help. Hamlet tells Horatio that he is dying and exchanges a last forgiveness with Laertes, who dies after absolving Hamlet.

The sound of marching echoes through the hall, and a shot rings out nearby. Osric declares that Fortinbras has come in conquest from Poland and now fires a volley to the English ambassadors. Hamlet tells Horatio again that he is dying, and urges his friend not to commit suicide in light of all the tragedies, but instead to stay alive and tell his story. He says that he wishes Fortinbras to be made King of Denmark; then he dies.

Fortinbras marches into the room accompanied by the English ambassadors, who announce that Rosencrantz and Guildenstern are dead. Horatio says that he will tell everyone assembled the story that led to the gruesome scene now on display. Fortinbras orders for Hamlet to be carried away like a soldier.

ANALYSIS

In the final scene, the violence, so long delayed, erupts with dizzying speed. Characters drop one after the other, poisoned, stabbed, and, in the case of Rosencrantz and Guildenstern, executed, as the theme of revenge and justice reaches its conclusion in the moment when Hamlet finally kills Claudius. In the moments before the duel, Hamlet seems peaceful, though also quite sad. He says that he feels ill in his heart, but he seems reconciled to the idea of death and no longer troubled by fear of the supernatural. Exactly what has caused the change in Hamlet is unclear, but his desire to attain Laertes' forgiveness clearly represents an important shift in his mental state. Whereas Hamlet previously was obsessed almost wholly with himself and his family, he is now able to think sympathetically about others. He does not go quite so far as to take responsibility for Polonius's death, but he does seem to be acting with a broader perspective after the shock of Ophelia's death. Hamlet's death at the hands of Laertes makes his earlier declaration over Polonius's corpse, that God has chosen "to punish me with this and this with me," prophetic (III.iv.174). His murder of Polonius does punish him in the end, since it is Laertes' vengeful rage over that murder that leads to Hamlet's death.

That death is neither heroic nor shameful, according to the moral logic of the play. Hamlet achieves his father's vengeance, but only after being spurred to it by the most extreme circumstances one might consider possible: watching his mother die and knowing that he, too, will die in moments.

The arrival of Fortinbras effectively poses the question of political legitimacy once again. In marked contrast to the corrupted and weakened royal family lying dead on the floor, Fortinbras clearly represents a strong-willed, capable leader, though the play does not address the question of whether his rule will restore the moral authority of the state.

IMPORTANT QUOTATIONS EXPLAINED

1. O that this too too solid flesh would melt,
    Thaw, and resolve itself into a dew!
    Or that the Everlasting had not fix'd
    His canon 'gainst self-slaughter! O God! O God!
    How weary, stale, flat, and unprofitable
    Seem to me all the uses of this world!
    Fie on't! O fie! 'tis an unweeded garden,
    That grows to seed; things rank and gross in nature
    Possess it merely. That it should come to this!
    But two months dead!—nay, not so much, not two:
    So excellent a king; that was, to this,
    Hyperion to a satyr; so loving to my mother,
    That he might not beteem the winds of heaven
    Visit her face too roughly. Heaven and earth!
    Must I remember? Why, she would hang on him
    As if increase of appetite had grown
    By what it fed on: and yet, within a month,—
    Let me not think on't,—Frailty, thy name is woman!—
    A little month; or ere those shoes were old
    With which she followed my poor father's body
    Like Niobe, all tears;—why she, even she,—
    O God! a beast that wants discourse of reason,
    Would have mourn'd longer,—married with mine uncle,
    My father's brother; but no more like my father
    Than I to Hercules: within a month;
    Ere yet the salt of most unrighteous tears
    Had left the flushing in her galled eyes,
    She married:— O, most wicked speed, to post
    With such dexterity to incestuous sheets!
    It is not, nor it cannot come to good;
    But break my heart,—for I must hold my tongue.

This quotation, Hamlet's first important soliloquy, occurs in Act I, scene ii (129–158). Hamlet speaks these lines after enduring the unpleasant scene at Claudius and Gertrude's court, then being asked by his mother and stepfather not to return to his studies at Wittenberg but to remain in Denmark, presumably against his wishes. Here, Hamlet thinks for the first time about suicide (desiring his flesh to "melt," and wishing that God had not made "self-slaughter" a sin), saying that the world is "weary, stale, flat, and unprofitable." In other words, suicide seems like a desirable alternative to life in a painful world, but Hamlet feels that the option of suicide is closed to him because it is forbidden by religion. Hamlet then goes on to describe the causes of his pain, specifically his intense disgust at his mother's marriage to Claudius. He describes the haste of their marriage, noting that the shoes his mother wore to his father's funeral were not worn out before her marriage to Claudius. He compares Claudius to his father (his father was "so excellent a king" while Claudius is a bestial "satyr"). As he runs through his description of their marriage, he touches upon the important motifs of misogyny, crying, "Frailty, thy name is woman"; incest, commenting that his mother moved "[w]ith such dexterity to incestuous sheets"; and the ominous omen the marriage represents for Denmark, that "[i]t is not nor it cannot come to good." Each of these motifs recurs throughout the play.

2. Give thy thoughts no tongue,
   Nor any unproportion'd thought his act.
   Be thou familiar, but by no means vulgar.
   Those friends thou hast, and their adoption tried,
   Grapple them unto thy soul with hoops of steel;
   But do not dull thy palm with entertainment
   Of each new-hatch'd, unfledg'd comrade. Beware
   Of entrance to a quarrel; but, being in,
   Bear't that the opposed may beware of thee.
   Give every man thine ear, but few thy voice:
   Take each man's censure, but reserve thy judgment.
   Costly thy habit as thy purse can buy,
   But not express'd in fancy; rich, not gaudy:
   For the apparel oft proclaims the man;
   And they in France of the best rank and station
   Are most select and generous chief in that.
   Neither a borrower nor a lender be:
   For loan oft loses both itself and friend;
   And borrowing dulls the edge of husbandry.
   This above all,—to thine own self be true;
   And it must follow, as the night the day,
   Thou canst not then be false to any man.

This famous bit of fatherly advice is spoken by Polonius to Laertes shortly before Laertes leaves for France, in Act I, scene iii (59–80). Polonius, who is bidding Laertes farewell, gives him this list of instructions about how to behave before he sends him on his way. His advice amounts to a list of clichés. Keep your thoughts to yourself; do not act rashly; treat people with familiarity but not excessively so; hold on to old friends and be slow to trust new friends; avoid fighting but fight boldly if it is unavoidable; be a good listener; accept criticism but do not be judgmental; maintain a proper appearance; do not borrow or lend money; and be true to yourself. This long list of quite normal fatherly advice emphasizes the regularity of Laertes' family life compared to Hamlet's, as well as contributing a somewhat stereotypical father-son encounter in the play's exploration of family relationships. It seems to indicate that Polonius loves his son, though that idea is complicated later in the play when he sends Reynaldo to spy on him.

QUOTATIONS

3.   Something is rotten in the state of Denmark.

This line is spoken by Marcellus in Act I, scene iv (67), as he and Horatio debate whether or not to follow Hamlet and the ghost into the dark night. The line refers both to the idea that the ghost is an ominous omen for Denmark and to the larger theme of the connection between the moral legitimacy of a ruler and the health of the state as a whole. The ghost is a visible symptom of the rottenness of Denmark created by Claudius's crime.

4.   I have of late,—but wherefore I know not,—lost all
     my mirth, forgone all custom of exercises; and indeed,
     it goes so heavily with my disposition that this goodly
     frame, the earth, seems to me a sterile promontory;
     this most excellent canopy, the air, look you, this
     brave o'erhanging firmament, this majestical roof
     fretted with golden fire,—why, it appears no other
     thing to me than a foul and pestilent congregation of
     vapours. What a piece of work is man! How noble in
     reason! how infinite in faculties! in form and moving,
     how express and admirable! in action how like an
     angel! in apprehension, how like a god! the beauty of
     the world! the paragon of animals! And yet, to me,
     what is this quintessence of dust?

In these lines, Hamlet speaks to Rosencrantz and Guildenstern in
Act II, scene ii (287–298), explaining the melancholy that has
afflicted him since his father's death. Perhaps moved by the presence
of his former university companions, Hamlet essentially engages in
a rhetorical exercise, building up an elaborate and glorified picture
of the earth and humanity before declaring it all merely a "quintes-
sence of dust." He examines the earth, the air, and the sun, and
rejects them as "a sterile promontory" and "a foul and pestilent
congregation of vapors." He then describes human beings from several perspectives, each one adding to his glorification of them.
Human beings' reason is noble, their faculties infinite, their forms
and movements fast and admirable, their actions angelic, and their
understanding godlike. But, to Hamlet, humankind is merely dust.
This motif, an expression of his obsession with the physicality of
death, recurs throughout the play, reaching its height in his speech
over Yorick's skull. Finally, it is also telling that Hamlet makes
humankind more impressive in "apprehension" (meaning understanding) than in "action." Hamlet himself is more prone to apprehension than to action, which is why he delays so long before
seeking his revenge on Claudius.

5.   To be, or not to be: that is the question:
     Whether 'tis nobler in the mind to suffer
     The slings and arrows of outrageous fortune
     Or to take arms against a sea of troubles,
     And by opposing end them?—To die,—to sleep,—
     No more; and by a sleep to say we end
     The heartache, and the thousand natural shocks
     That flesh is heir to,—'tis a consummation
     Devoutly to be wish'd. To die,—to sleep;—
     To sleep: perchance to dream:—ay, there's the rub;
     For in that sleep of death what dreams may come,
     When we have shuffled off this mortal coil,
     Must give us pause: there's the respect
     That makes calamity of so long life;
     For who would bear the whips and scorns of time,
     The oppressor's wrong, the proud man's contumely,
     The pangs of despis'd love, the law's delay,
     The insolence of office, and the spurns
     That patient merit of the unworthy takes,
     When he himself might his quietus make
     With a bare bodkin? who would these fardels bear,
     To grunt and sweat under a weary life,
     But that the dread of something after death,—
     The undiscover'd country, from whose bourn
     No traveller returns,—puzzles the will,
     And makes us rather bear those ills we have
     Than fly to others that we know not of?
     Thus conscience does make cowards of us all;
     And thus the native hue of resolution
     Is sicklied o'er with the pale cast of thought;
     And enterprises of great pith and moment,
     With this regard, their currents turn awry,
     And lose the name of action.

This soliloquy, probably the most famous speech in the English language, is spoken by Hamlet in Act III, scene i (58–90). His most logical and powerful examination of the theme of the moral legitimacy of suicide in an unbearably painful world, it touches on several of the other important themes of the play. Hamlet poses the problem of whether to commit suicide as a logical question: "To be, or not to be," that is, to live or not to live. He then weighs the moral ramifications of living and dying. Is it nobler to suffer life, "[t]he slings and arrows of outrageous fortune," passively or to actively seek to end one's suffering? He compares death to sleep and thinks of the end to suffering, pain, and uncertainty it might bring, "[t]he heartache, and the thousand natural shocks / That flesh is heir to." Based on this metaphor, he decides that suicide is a desirable course of action, "a consummation / Devoutly to be wished." But, as the religious word "devoutly" signifies, there is more to the question, namely, what will happen in the afterlife. Hamlet immediately realizes as much, and he reconfigures his metaphor of sleep to include the possibility of dreaming; he says that the dreams that may come in the sleep of death are daunting, that they "must give us pause."

He then decides that the uncertainty of the afterlife, which is intimately related to the theme of the difficulty of attaining truth in a spiritually ambiguous world, is essentially what prevents all of humanity from committing suicide to end the pain of life. He outlines a long list of the miseries of experience, ranging from lovesickness to hard work to political oppression, and asks who would choose to bear those miseries if he could bring himself peace with a knife, "[w]hen he himself might his quietus make / With a bare bodkin?" He answers himself again, saying no one would choose to live, except that "the dread of something after death" makes people submit to the suffering of their lives rather than go to another state of existence which might be even more miserable. The dread of the afterlife, Hamlet concludes, leads to excessive moral sensitivity that makes action impossible: "conscience does make cowards of us all . . . thus the native hue of resolution / Is sicklied o'er with the pale cast of thought."

In this way, this speech connects many of the play's main themes, including the idea of suicide and death, the difficulty of knowing the truth in a spiritually ambiguous universe, and the connection between thought and action. In addition to its crucial thematic content, this speech is important for what it reveals about the quality of Hamlet's mind. His deeply passionate nature is complemented by a relentlessly logical intellect, which works furiously to find a solution to his misery. He has turned to religion and found it inadequate to help him either kill himself or resolve to kill Claudius. Here, he turns to a logical philosophical inquiry and finds it equally frustrating.

KEY FACTS

FULL TITLE
The Tragedy of Hamlet, Prince of Denmark

AUTHOR
William Shakespeare

TYPE OF WORK
Drama

GENRE
Revenge tragedy

LANGUAGE
English

TIME AND PLACE WRITTEN
London, England, early seventeenth century
(probably 1600–1602)

DATE OF FIRST PUBLICATION
1603, in a pirated quarto edition titled *The Tragicall Historie of
Hamlet*; 1604 in a superior quarto edition

NARRATOR
None

NONCLIMAX
The duel between Hamlet and Laertes in Act V, scene ii, which
leads to the deaths of Hamlet, Laertes, Claudius, and Gertrude

PROTAGONIST
Hamlet

ANTAGONIST
Claudius

SETTINGS (TIME)
The late medieval period, though the play's chronological
setting is notoriously imprecise

SETTINGS (PLACE)
Denmark

POINT OF VIEW
Mainly Hamlet's

FALLING ACTION
Fortinbras's arrival at Elsinore after the deaths of the royal family in Act V, scene ii

TENSE
Present

FORESHADOWING
The ghost, which is taken to foreshadow an ominous future for Denmark

TONES
Dark, ironic, melancholy, passionate, contemplative, desperate, violent

THEMES
The impossibility of certainty; the complexity of action; the mystery of death; the nation as a diseased body

MOTIFS
Incest and incestuous desire; ears and hearing; death and suicide; darkness and the supernatural; misogyny

SYMBOLS
The ghost (the spiritual consequences of death); Yorick's skull (the physical consequences of death)

Study Questions & Essay Topics

Study Questions

1. *Shakespeare includes characters in* Hamlet *who are obvious foils for Hamlet, including, most obviously, Horatio, Fortinbras, Claudius, and Laertes. Compare and contrast Hamlet with each of these characters. How are they alike? How are they different? How does each respond to the crises with which he is faced?*

Horatio's steadfastness and loyalty contrasts with Hamlet's variability and excitability, though both share a love of learning, reason, and thought. Claudius's willingness to disregard all moral law and act decisively to fulfill his appetites and lust for power contrasts powerfully with Hamlet's concern for morality and indecisive inability to act. Fortinbras's willingness to go to great lengths to avenge his father's death, even to the point of waging war, contrasts sharply with Hamlet's inactivity, even though both of them are concerned with avenging their fathers. Laertes' single-minded, furious desire to avenge Polonius stands in stark opposition to Hamlet's inactivity with regard to his own father's death. Finally, Hamlet, Laertes, and Fortinbras are all in a position to seek revenge for the murders of their fathers, and their situations are deeply intertwined. Hamlet's father killed Fortinbras's father, and Hamlet killed Laertes' father, meaning that Hamlet occupies the same role for Laertes as Claudius does for Hamlet.

2.   *Many critics take a deterministic view of* Hamlet's *plot,
      arguing that the prince's inability to act and tendency
      toward melancholy reflection is a "tragic flaw" that leads
      inevitably to his demise. Is this an accurate way of
      understanding the play? Why or why not? Given
      Hamlet's character and situation, would another outcome
      of the play have been possible?*

The idea of the "tragic flaw" is a problematic one in *Hamlet*. It is
true that Hamlet possesses definable characteristics that, by shaping
his behavior, contribute to his tragic fate. But to argue that his tragedy is inevitable because he possesses these characteristics is difficult
to prove. Given a scenario and a description of the characters
involved, it is highly unlikely that anyone who had not read or seen
Hamlet would be able to predict its ending based solely on the character of its hero. In fact, the play's chaotic train of events suggests
that human beings are forced to make choices whose consequences
are unforeseeable as well as unavoidable. To argue that the play's
outcome is intended to appear inevitable seems incompatible with
the thematic claims made by the play itself.

3.   *Throughout the play, Hamlet claims to be feigning
     madness, but his portrayal of a madman is so intense and
     so convincing that many readers believe that Hamlet
     actually slips into insanity at certain moments in the play.
     Do you think this is true, or is Hamlet merely play-acting
     insanity? What evidence can you cite for either claim?*

At any given moment during the play, the most accurate assessment
of Hamlet's state of mind probably lies somewhere between sanity
and insanity. Hamlet certainly displays a high degree of mania and
instability throughout much of the play, but his "madness" is perhaps too purposeful and pointed for us to conclude that he actually
loses his mind. His language is erratic and wild, but beneath his
mad-sounding words often lie acute observations that show the
sane mind working bitterly beneath the surface. Most likely, Hamlet's decision to feign madness is a sane one, taken to confuse his
enemies and hide his intentions.

On the other hand, Hamlet finds himself in a unique and traumatic situation, one which calls into question the basic truths and
ideals of his life. He can no longer believe in religion, which has
failed his father and doomed him to life amid miserable experience.
He can no longer trust society, which is full of hypocrisy and violence, nor love, which has been poisoned by his mother's betrayal of
his father's memory. And, finally, he cannot turn to philosophy,
which cannot explain ghosts or answer his moral questions and lead
him to action.

With this much discord in his mind, and already under the
extraordinary pressure of grief from his father's death, his mother's
marriage, and the responsibility bequeathed to him by the ghost,
Hamlet is understandably distraught. He may not be mad, but he
likely is close to the edge of sanity during many of the most intense
moments in the play, such as during the performance of the play-
within-a-play (III.ii), his confrontation with Ophelia (III.i), and his
long confrontation with his mother (III.iv).

SUGGESTED ESSAY TOPICS

1. Think about Hamlet's relationship with Ophelia. Does he love her? Does he stop loving her? Did he ever love her? What evidence can you find in the play to support your opinion?

2. Consider Rosencrantz and Guildenstern's role in the play. Why might Shakespeare have created characters like this? Are they there for comic relief, or do they serve a more serious purpose? Why does the news of their deaths come only after the deaths of the royal family in Act V, as if this news were not anticlimactic? Is it acceptable for Hamlet to treat them as he does? Why or why not?

3. Analyze the use of descriptions and images in *Hamlet*. How does Shakespeare use descriptive language to enhance the visual possibilities of a stage production? How does he use imagery to create a mood of tension, suspense, fear, and despair?

4. Analyze the use of comedy in *Hamlet*, paying particular attention to the gravediggers, Osric, and Polonius. Does comedy serve merely to relieve the tension of the tragedy, or do the comic scenes serve a more serious thematic purpose as well?

5. Suicide is an important theme in *Hamlet*. Discuss how the play treats the idea of suicide morally, religiously, and aesthetically, with particular attention to Hamlet's two important statements about suicide: the "O, that this too too solid flesh would melt" soliloquy (I.ii.129–158) and the "To be, or not to be" soliloquy (III.i.56–88). Why does Hamlet believe that, although capable of suicide, most human beings choose to live, despite the cruelty, pain, and injustice of the world?

QUESTIONS & ESSAYS

REVIEW & RESOURCES

QUIZ

1. Whom does Polonius send to France to spy on Laertes?

   A. Reynaldo
   B. Ophelia
   C. Guido
   D. Marcellus

2. Where does the ghost appear during the play?

   A. The castle ramparts and the great hall of Elsinore
   B. Fortinbras's tent and Hamlet's bedchamber
   C. The castle ramparts and Gertrude's bedchamber
   D. Gertrude's bedchamber and the great hall of Elsinore

3. How did Claudius murder King Hamlet?

   A. By stabbing him through an arras
   B. By pouring poison into his ear
   C. By ordering him to be hanged
   D. By poisoning his wineglass

4. Where is the university at which Horatio and Hamlet studied?

   A. Paris
   B. Oxford
   C. Constantinople
   D. Wittenberg

5. Whose skull does Hamlet discover in the churchyard?

   A. The former court jester's
   B. Reynaldo's
   C. Ophelia's
   D. His father's

6. Which of the following characters cannot see the ghost?

    A. Marcellus
    B. Hamlet
    C. Gertrude
    D. Horatio

7. Who escorts Hamlet on the voyage to England?

    A. Cornelius and Voltimand
    B. Rosencrantz and Guildenstern
    C. Marcellus and Bernardo
    D. Captain Vicissus and the one-eyed thief

8. Where do Hamlet and Laertes fight during Ophelia's funeral?

    A. In the nearby woods
    B. Beside Ophelia's grave
    C. Inside the church
    D. Inside the grave itself

9. Which of the following characters survive the play?

    A. Fortinbras, Horatio, and Osric
    B. Prince Hamlet, Polonius, and Gertrude
    C. Claudius, Rosencrantz, and Guildenstern
    D. Ophelia, Laertes, and King Hamlet

10. What does Hamlet claim to be able to tell the difference between when the wind is from the south?

    A. A flea and a fire log
    B. A nymph and a nihilist
    C. A hawk and a handsaw
    D. A shark and St. Timothy

11. In whose history of Denmark did Shakespeare find background material for his play?

    A. Oedipus of Thebes
    B. Saxo Grammaticus
    C. Franz Guntherhaasen
    D. Dionysus Finn

12. How does Ophelia die?

    A. Claudius stabs her
    B. Hamlet strangles her
    C. She slits her wrists
    D. She drowns in the river

13. Whose story does Hamlet ask the players to tell upon their arrival to Elsinore?

    A. Priam and Hecuba's
    B. Antony and Cleopatra's
    C. Gertrude and Claudius's
    D. His father's

14. Why, according to Polonius, has Hamlet gone mad?

    A. He grieves too much for his father
    B. He despises Claudius for marrying Gertrude
    C. He is in love with Ophelia
    D. He is jealous of Laertes and longs to return to Wittenberg

15. Who is the last character to die in the play?

    A. Horatio
    B. Hamlet
    C. Claudius
    D. Fortinbras

16. How many characters die during the course of the play?

    A. Two
    B. Five
    C. Seven
    D. Eight

17. Who speaks the famous "To be, or not to be" soliloquy?

    A. Claudius
    B. Hamlet
    C. The ghost
    D. Laertes

REVIEW & RESOURCES

18. In what country do Rosencrantz and Guildenstern die?

    A.   Belgium
    B.   Denmark
    C.   England
    D.   Poland

19. Why does Hamlet decide not to kill Claudius after the traveling players' play?

    A.   Claudius is praying
    B.   Claudius is asleep
    C.   Claudius pleads for mercy
    D.   Gertrude is in the next room

20. Who killed Fortinbras's father?

    A.   Prince Hamlet
    B.   Laertes
    C.   Fortinbras
    D.   Hamlet's father

21. Which character speaks the first line of the play?

    A.   Bernardo
    B.   Francisco
    C.   Hamlet
    D.   Horatio

22. In which of the following years was Hamlet most likely written?

    A.   1570
    B.   1601
    C.   1581
    D.   1610

23. Which of Claudius and Laertes' traps for Hamlet succeeds in killing him?

    A.   The poisoned cup
    B.   The sharpened sword
    C.   The poisoned dagger
    D.   The poisoned sword

24. Which character speaks from beneath the stage toward the end of Act I?

    A. The Ghost
    B. Hamlet
    C. Claudius
    D. Polonius

25. Who returns Hamlet to Denmark after his exile?

    A. Horatio
    B. Claudius
    C. A group of pirates
    D. A group of monks

SUGGESTIONS FOR FURTHER READING

BLOOM, HAROLD. *Shakespeare: The Invention of the Human.* New York: Riverhead Books, 1998.

BRADLEY, A. C. *Shakespearean Tragedy: Lectures on* HAMLET, OTHELLO, KING LEAR *&* MACBETH. New York: Penguin, 1991.

ELIOT, THOMAS STERNS. "Hamlet and His Problems." In *The Sacred Wood.* London: Methuen, 1920.

FRYE, NORTHROP. *Fools of Time: Studies in Shakespearean Tragedy.* Toronto: University of Toronto Press, 1967.

GREENBLATT, STEPHEN. *Hamlet in Purgatory.* Princeton: Princeton University Press, 2001.

LEVIN, HARRY. *The Question of* HAMLET. New York: Oxford University Press, 1959.

WILSON, JOHN DOVER. *What Happens in* HAMLET. New York: Cambridge University Press, 1951.

SPARKNOTES
TEST PREPARATION
GUIDES

The SparkNotes team figured it was time to cut standardized tests down to size. We've studied the tests for you, so that SparkNotes test prep guides are:

Smarter:
Packed with critical-thinking skills and test-
taking strategies that will improve your score.

Better:
Fully up to date, covering all new features of the tests,
with study tips on every type of question.

Faster:
Our books cover exactly what you need to
know for the test. No more, no less.

SPARKNOTES STUDY GUIDES: